My Victory-Filled Day

Harrison House

Shippensburg, PA

A *Sparkling Gems from the Greek*
Guided Devotional Journal

My Victory-
Filled
Day

Rick Renner

Published by Harrison House Publishers
Shippensburg, PA 17257

ISBN 13 TP: 978-1-6675-1133-7

ISBN 13 eBook: 978-1-6675-1134-4

For Worldwide Distribution, Printed in the U.S.A.

1 2 3 4 5 6 7 8 / 29 28 27 26 25

Contents

Day 1

Spiritual Warfare Is Real!

> *For we wrestle not against flesh and blood, but against principalities, against powers, against the rulers of the darkness of this world, against spiritual wickedness in high places.*
>
> — Ephesians 6:12

Spiritual warfare is real! The devil and his demon spirits are not myths or fantasies. These are real beings that hate the human race and therefore roam about seeking whom they might destroy and devour. That's why it is vitally important to know how to best protect yourself against their attacks!

Most of the attacks the devil wages against you will occur in your mind. He knows that your mind is the central control center for your life; therefore, if he can take control of one small area of your mind, he can begin to expand outward into other weak areas that need to be strengthened by the Holy Spirit and the Word of God. By poisoning your mind with unbelief and lying strongholds, the devil can then manipulate not only your mind, but also your emotions and your body. There is no doubt about it — the mind is the strategic center where the battle is won or lost in spiritual warfare!

The devil wants to get access into your life — and if he finds that access, you may be headed for quite a conflict! You can see why it is so important that you keep every door shut; then the enemy won't be able to find any entrance through which he can begin to wage warfare against you.

However, the devil will often put up quite a fight even when he *doesn't* find an entrance into our lives. That's why we need to know exactly what the Bible says about spiritual warfare.

In Ephesians 6:12, Paul told us, "For we wrestle not against flesh and blood, but against principalities, against powers, against the rulers of the darkness of this world, against spiritual wickedness in high places." I want to especially draw your attention to the word "wrestle" in this verse, for this word is the key to understanding how intense spiritual warfare can become!

The word "wrestle" is from the old Greek word *pale,* which refers to *struggling, wrestling,* or *hand-to-hand combat.* However, the word pale is also the Greek word from which the Greeks derived their name for the *Palaestra* — a huge palace of combat sports that was situated in the center of most larger, ancient cities.

The Palaestra was a huge building that outwardly looked like a palace but was dedicated to the cultivation of athletic skills. Every morning, afternoon, and night, the most committed, determined, and daring athletes of the day could be found in this fabulous building, working out and training for their respective sports. Three kinds of athletes primarily worked out at the Palaestra: *boxers, wrestlers,* and *pankratists.*

Let me tell you a little about how these sports functioned in the First Century when Paul wrote this verse, because it forms the backdrop to the word "wrestle" in Ephesians 6:12. The first and most feared combat sport was *boxing*. But the boxers from the First Century were not like our boxers today. Their sport was *extremely violent* — so violent that they were not permitted to box without wearing helmets. Without the protection of helmets, their heads would have been *crushed!* In fact, this sport was so severe that few boxers ever lived to retire from their profession. Most of them died in the ring. Of all the sports, the ancients viewed boxing as the most hazardous and deadly.

In this brutal and barbaric sport, the ancient boxers wore gloves ribbed with steel and spiked with nails. At times the steel wrapped around their gloves was serrated, like the blade of a hunting knife, in order to make deep gashes in the opponent's skin. In addition to this, they used extremely heavy gloves that made every punch more damaging. It is quite usual to find artwork from the time of the ancient Greeks that includes boxers whose faces, ears, and noses are totally deformed from being struck by these dangerous gloves.

Making this sport even more dangerous was the fact that there were *no rules* — except that a boxer couldn't clench his opponent's fist. That was the only rule of the game! There were no "rounds" like there are in boxing today. The fight just went on and on until one of the two surrendered or died in the ring.

Next, there were *wrestlers!* Wrestling was the most ancient of the combat sports. Because it was an essential part of the education of Roman boys in the wealthier classes, every adult male in those classes learned to wrestle. However, combat-sport wrestling was *very* different than simple wrestling.

Although not quite as ugly and bloody as the other two combat sports, combat wrestling was still very aggressive and dangerous. Certain rules applied to the competitions of this combat sport. For instance, some of the most violent fighting techniques weren't allowed in wrestling, such as blows, kicks, thrusts, throttle holds, twisting of the joints, and fighting on the ground.

The third combat sport was *pankration,* from the Greek words *pan* and *kratos.* The word *pan* means *all*, and *kration* is from the word *kratos,* which means *power.* When these two words were put together, they formed the word *pankration,* which means *all powerful.* These fighters were the fiercest, toughest, and most committed of all! In this sport, they were permitted to kick, punch, bite, gouge, strike, break fingers, break legs, and to do any other horrible thing you could imagine. There was no part of the human body that was off limits. They could do anything they wanted to any part of their competitor's body, for there were basically no rules.

An early inscription from a father to his sons who participated in pankration says this: "If you should hear your son has died, you can believe it. But if you hear he has been defeated and chose to retire, do not believe it!" Why? Because like the other combat sports, pankration was *extremely violent.* While participating in this sport, more professional pankratists died than surrendered or were simply defeated.

I realize that these are very graphic images, but they are also very important images, for they are all contained in the word "wrestle" that Paul uses in Ephesians 6:12. In the day when Paul wrote this letter, everyone who saw the Greek word *pale* ("wrestle") saw all these images in their minds. You can see, then, that this was a powerful, pungent word for Paul to use when he started to describe our conflict with unseen, demonic powers that Satan has marshaled together to try to destroy us. By using the word "wrestle" from the Greek word *pale,* Paul was telling every reader (and us) that spiritual warfare can be a *bitter struggle* and *an intense conflict.*

This first phrase in Ephesians 6:12 really carries this idea:

"For our wrestling — that is, our intense struggle, fierce combat, contest, challenge, and ongoing conflict — is not really with flesh and blood, but with...."

Then Paul goes on to describe the different levels of demonic powers that exist in Satan's kingdom. As we look at what Paul said, I want you to see that this conflict can be fierce! I don't mean to alarm you, but you need to know that the devil is serious in his attempts to destroy you — and if you haven't prepared yourself spiritually to thwart such attacks, you may find yourself in a real quandary.

You see, our adversary is real. There are foul forces of darkness that work covertly behind most disasters and many moral failures. *However, these demonic spirits can't do anything unless our flesh cooperates with them!* They may come to tempt, to seduce, to deceive, and to assault the mind — but unless they find a partner to listen or cooperate with them, their evil attempts are futile and powerless.

Therefore, the greatest key to winning every battle the devil wages against you is to keep your mind dominated by the Word of God. As you do that, your flesh will be kept under the control of the Holy Spirit, which will block the majority of the enemy's attacks against your mind! This is why Peter urges us to "...gird up the loins of your mind..." (1 Peter 1:13).

Remember, the devil knows that if he can take control of one small area of your mind, he can begin to expand outward into other weak areas of your life. Therefore, don't you think it's time for you to start reading your Bible and filling your mind with God's thoughts? There is no better mental protection against the enemy's strategies than to fill your brain with God's Word! It will strengthen you and keep your mind free from unbelief and lying strongholds.

So take God's Word deep into your mind, and stop the devil from finding access into your life. Do everything you can to shut every door. Don't give the enemy any entrance through which he can begin to wage warfare against you!

My Prayer for Today

Lord, I don't want to ever give the devil access to my mind. I ask for forgiveness for the times I've permitted wrong thinking to go on inside me when I knew it was wrong. Now I understand that these are the areas through which the devil seeks to find entrance into my life. Starting today, I am asking You to help me locate each "open door" in my mind; then help me seal those doors shut by the power of Your Spirit and Your Word! I pray this in Jesus' name!

My Confession for Today

I confess that my mind is dominated by the Word of God and that I am under the control of the Holy Spirit! I gird up the loins of my mind by reading my Bible and filling my mind with God's thoughts. God's Word strengthens me and keeps my mind free from unbelief and lying strongholds. I take God's Word deep into my mind, and it stops the devil from finding access into my life! I declare this by faith in Jesus' name!

Questions for You to Consider

1. Can you think of any "open doors" in your mind right now through which the devil finds access into your life? Write down the "open doors" you need to shut immediately in order to stop the enemy's attacks.

_____

_____

_____

_____

_____

_____

2. Now that you have identified these areas, what are you going to do to seal them shut so the devil's access to your life is stopped?

_____

_____

_____

_____

_____

_____

3. Are you able to do this on your own, or do you need to ask someone to help you with prayer and daily encouragement? If you need help, ask the Holy Spirit to show you whom you should talk to. Then boldly go to that person and ask for his or her assistance.

_____

_____

_____

_____

_____

_____

Day 2

The Rank and File of Satan's Kingdom

For we wrestle not against flesh and blood, but against principalities, against powers, against the rulers of the darkness of this world, against spiritual wickedness in high places.

— Ephesians 6:12

I realize that many people tend to think that screaming, yelling, screeching, stomping, and shouting are required to defeat the devil. However, these actions will accomplish nothing if those same people are not living a consecrated and holy life.

It is simply a fact that if we have deliberately or by negligence allowed sinful strongholds to secretly remain in our lives, then we have left gaping holes through which Satan may continue to insert his schemes into our lives. Negligence in dealing with these secret places may give Satan the very loopholes he needs to orchestrate our defeat!

This business of spiritual warfare is serious! We must do all we can to shut every door to our souls through which the devil might attempt to access our lives. Because this issue is so serious, we would do well to pay attention when the Bible offers us information about the enemy of our souls. The devil has destroyed too many Christians who were ignorant of his devices!

In Ephesians 6:12, the apostle Paul presents a divine revelation he received that describes how Satan's kingdom has been militarily aligned. He writes, "For we wrestle not against flesh and blood, but against principalities, against powers, against the rulers of the darkness of this world, against spiritual wickedness in high places."

Notice that at the top of this list, Paul mentions a group of evil spirits he calls "principalities." This word is taken from the Greek word *archai,* an old word that is used symbolically to denote *ancient times.* It is also used to depict *individuals who hold the highest and loftiest position of rank and authority*. By using the word *archai,* Paul emphatically tells us that at the very top of Satan's kingdom are powerful evil beings that have held their lofty positions of power and authority since ancient times — probably ever since the fall of Lucifer.

Paul goes on to tell us that below principalities is a second group of evil beings he refers to as "powers." This word "powers" is taken from the Greek word *exousia,* and it denotes *delegated authority*. This describes a lower, second-level group of evil beings — demon spirits — who have received *delegated authority* from Satan to carry out all manner of evil in whatever way they desire to do it. These evil forces are second in command in Satan's dark kingdom.

Continuing in his description of Satan's rank and file in descending order, Paul mentions "the rulers of the darkness of this world." This amazing phrase is taken from the word *kosmokrateros* and is a compound of the words *kosmos* and *kratos.* The word *kosmos* denotes *order* or *arrangement,* whereas the word *kratos* has to do with *raw power*. Thus, the compounded word *kosmokrateros* depicts *raw power that has been harnessed and put into some kind of order.*

This word *kosmokrateros* was at times used to picture *military training camps where young men were assembled, trained, and turned into a mighty army.* These young men were like raw power when they first arrived in the training camp. However, as the military training progressed and the new recruits were taught discipline and order, all that raw manpower was converted into an organized, disciplined army. This is the word Paul now uses in his description of Satan's kingdom. *What does it mean?*

It tells you and me that Satan is so serious about doing damage to the human race that he deals with demon spirits as though they are *troops!* He puts them in rank and file, gives them orders and assignments, and then sends them out like military soldiers who are committed to kill. Just as men in a human army are equipped and trained in their methods of destruction, so, too, are these demon spirits. And once these demons are trained and ready to start their assault, Satan sends them forth to do their devious work against human beings.

Paul makes reference to this dispatch of evil spirits when he writes next about "spiritual wickedness in high places." The word "wickedness" is taken from the word *poneros,* and it is used to depict *something that is bad, vile, malevolent, vicious, impious, and malignant.* This tells us the ultimate aim of Satan's dark domain: These evil spirits are sent forth to afflict humanity in *bad, vile, malevolent, and vicious ways!*

Satan uses all these evil forces in his attacks against mankind. Nevertheless, we believers have far more authority and power than the devil and his forces. You and I have the Greater One living within us! As members of the Church of Jesus Christ, we are loaded with heaps and heaps of raw power, for the Church has no shortage of power, nor is it deficient in God-given authority. We have more power and more authority than all these evil forces combined!

What we lack is *order* and *discipline*. We must learn to see ourselves as the army of God and to view the local church as the training center where we are taught to do God's business. Then we must heed the call of Jesus and be dispatched into the dark world to preach the Gospel and to drive these evil forces from people's lives. We must buckle down and begin to view ourselves as the troops of Jesus Christ!

Being organized and disciplined includes living a holy and consecrated life. There is no room for slackness in the life of a real Christian soldier. To deal with these forces that are being dispatched to destroy us and the world around us, it is required that we walk with God and listen to the voice of His Spirit. We must gird up the loins of our minds and fill our thoughts with the Word of God. Satan's troops are serious — and if we're not serious about our contest with them, it will only be a matter of time until they discover our weakness and strike with all their force to bring us down.

Determine to see yourself as a soldier in the army of God. Don't allow *anything* to remain in your life that would hinder your fight of faith. Be disciplined, committed, and organized. Take advantage of all the weapons described in Ephesians 6:13-18. *Then get ready to witness the awesome demonstration of God's power in your life as you prevail against Satan's rank and file!*

My Prayer for Today

Lord, help me start seeing myself as a mighty soldier in the army of God. You have provided every weapon I need to prevail against the enemies that come against my life, my family, my business, my friends, and my church. I want to stand tall and firm against the wicked plots the devil tries to exert against people's lives whom I love and need. Holy Spirit, give me the power and strength I need to successfully resist every attack and to drive all dark forces from my life and from the lives of those close to me! I pray this in Jesus' name!

My Confession for Today

I confess that I live a holy and consecrated life! There is no room for slackness in my life. I am serious about serving God as a real Christian soldier. I do everything that is required for me to walk with God and to hear the voice of His Spirit when He speaks to me. I am very serious about winning every conflict with evil forces. Because of my strong commitment to this fight of faith, I am more than a match for anything the devil tries to throw at me! I declare this by faith in Jesus' name!

Questions for You to Consider

1. What did you learn by reading this Sparkling Gem?

    _____
    _____
    _____
    _____
    _____
    _____

2. Do you see yourself as a soldier in the army of God?

    _____
    _____
    _____
    _____
    _____
    _____

3. Do you view your local church as a place for you to be trained, taught, and disciplined in order to become a better Christian soldier?

_____

_____

_____

_____

_____

_____

Day 3

Don't Ignore the Last Words!

> *Finally, my brethren, be strong in the Lord, and in the power of his might.*
>
> — Ephesians 6:10

In the sixth chapter of Ephesians, the apostle Paul writes his great text about spiritual warfare and spiritual weapons. But before Paul goes into a detailed explanation of our spiritual armor, he first passionately beseeches us, "Finally, my brethren, be strong in the Lord...."

The word "finally" is one of the most important words in this text. It is taken from the Greek phrase *tou loipou* and would be better translated *for the rest of the matter; in conclusion; or in summation.* The phrase *tou loipou* is used in other Greek manuscripts of that same period to depict something so extremely important that it is placed at the very end of the letter. This way if the reader remembers nothing else in the letter, he will be more likely to remember this one thing.

With this in mind, the word "finally" in Ephesians 6:10 carries this idea:

"In conclusion, I have saved the most important issue of this epistle until the end of the letter, so if you remember nothing else I have said, you will remember this. I want this to stand out in your mind...!"

This is a remarkable statement! The book of Ephesians contains some of the deepest theological teaching in the New Testament. Let me mention just a few of these theological points. Paul writes about:

- The election of the saints (Ephesians 1:4)

- The predestination work of God (Ephesians 1:5)

- The adoption of the sons of God (Ephesians 1:5)

- The dispensation of the fullness of times (Ephesians 1:10)

- The sealing of the Holy Spirit (Ephesians 1:13)

- The earnest of the Holy Spirit (Ephesians 1:14)

- The power of God that is available to every believer (Ephesians 1:19)

- The grace of God (Ephesians 2:1-10)

- The eternal plan of God (Ephesians 3:10-11)

- The fivefold ministry gifts (Ephesians 4:11-13)

- The infilling with the Spirit (Ephesians 5:18-19)

- *And the list goes on and on.*

But in addition to these important theological points, the book of Ephesians also includes some of the most practical instructions in the New Testament regarding such issues as:

- The relationship between believers (Ephesians 4:25-5:2)

- The relationship between believers and the world (Ephesians 5:3-16)

- The relationship between husbands and wives (Ephesians 5:22-33)

- The relationship between parents and children (Ephesians 6:1-4)

- The relationship between employers and employees (Ephesians 6:5-9)

Yet when you come to the end of this epistle that is so jam-packed with theological and practical truths, Paul says, "Finally..." and then begins to speak to us about *spiritual warfare!*

Why is this? Because like so many in the Church world today, the Ephesian believers had gathered together a vast accumulation of spiritual knowledge, information, and facts; nevertheless, this alone was not enough to keep the devil under their feet where he belonged! As we read through chapter 4, we can see that the devil was apparently attacking the Ephesian church and was having some success!

That's why Paul had to instruct these believers to put away lying, steal no more, let no corrupt communication out of their mouths, grieve not the Holy Spirit, and put aside all anger and malice (Ephesians 4:25-31). Does this sound like a church full of victorious people to you? The Ephesian believers were members of the largest church of that day, yet they were not fully experiencing the overcoming, abundant life that Jesus Christ had come to offer them.

Consider your own life. Are you experiencing victory in most areas of your life, or are you suffering defeat in key areas? Have you ignored the fact that spiritual warfare is real? Have you gathered lots of spiritual information, knowledge, and facts, yet forgotten to put on the whole armor of God?

Praise God for all the knowledge you've gained, but now it's time to turn your intellectual knowledge of God's Word into the sword of the Spirit. Then you must raise it high and brandish it against the onslaughts the enemy has been trying to bring against you. It's also time for you to turn your knowledge about faith into a shield that withstands every demonic attack! That's why Paul said, "Finally...." In case the Ephesian believers didn't remember anything else, he wanted them to remember that they *had* to have spiritual weapons to keep the devil under their feet.

How about you? Are you dressed in the whole armor of God today?

My Prayer for Today

Lord, help me not to get so brain-heavy with facts, knowledge, and information that I forget I must have more than brain power. I am asking You to help me focus on my spiritual side and to stay equipped with the spiritual weapons You have provided for me, for I know that knowledge alone is not enough to keep the devil under my feet. Today I choose to pick up those weapons and to walk in the whole armor of God! I pray this in Jesus' name!

My Confession for Today

I confess that I have spiritual weapons to defeat the enemy! I walk in those weapons and use them every time the devil tries to attack my life or the lives of those I love. Because I have the whole armor of God, I am fit and equipped to shove back every assault the devil may try to bring against me. God has more than adequately outfitted me with every weapon I need to maintain the victory Jesus obtained for me. I declare this by faith in Jesus' name!

Questions for You to Consider

1. When you take a serious look at your life, do you think you're doing all you can to keep the devil out of your affairs?

_____

_____

_____

_____

_____

_____

2. Are there any areas of your life that are "targets" for the devil right now because of something you're doing that you shouldn't be doing?

_____

_____

_____

_____

_____

_____

3. How long has it been since you read Ephesians 6:10-18 and really meditated on those verses about spiritual weapons? Don't you think you should take some time to do it today?

_____

_____

_____

_____

_____

_____

Day 4

It's Time for You To Stop Acting Like You're a Victim!

> *And having spoiled principalities and powers, he made a shew of them openly, triumphing over them in it.*
>
> — Colossians 2:15

We can count on the fact that there are unseen evil forces that have been assigned to kill, steal, and destroy everything good in our lives. The Bible clearly teaches that these devilish forces band together to commit acts of aggression against the saints — and that includes you and me!

This truth is quite evident in Scripture, for Paul wrote many verses about spiritual weapons, spiritual armor, and how we are to resist these unseen, demonic forces. Yet it is *very important* that we approach this subject with the right attitude!

Because of Jesus' death on the Cross and His resurrection from the dead, the forces of hell are *already* defeated. However, even though they have been legally stripped of their authority and power, they continue to roam around this earth, carrying out evil deeds like criminals, bandits, hooligans, and thugs. And just like criminals who refuse to submit to the law, these evil spirits will continue to operate in this world until some believer uses his God-given authority to enforce their defeat!

We need to get ahold of this truth: These demonic forces are legally stripped of their authority and are defeated! We are not puny, struggling believers who are somehow trying to learn how to cope with the devil's attacks against us. We're not merely trying to learn how to scrape by or survive. Jesus' death and resurrection gave us the legal authority to keep Satan under our feet, so we must always make sure we approach spiritual warfare as *victors* and not *victims*.

Let's look at Colossians 2:15 to gain a greater revelation of the victory Jesus has already accomplished for you and me through His death, burial, and resurrection. Paul tells us that Jesus "...made a shew of them *openly*...." The word "openly" is taken from the word *parresia,* a word that is used throughout the books of the New Testament to denote *boldness* or *confidence.*

By using the word *parresia,* Paul declares that when Jesus was finishing His dealings with Satan, His victory over the devil was no "quiet affair." Quite the contrary! Jesus *boldly, confidently,* and *loudly* exposed and displayed this now-defunct foe to Heaven's hosts. Make no mistake! When Jesus "made a shew of them openly," it was quite a spectacular show!

The verse continues, "...He made a shew of them openly, *triumphing over them in it."* The word "triumph" is taken from the Greek word *triambeuo,* which is a technical word used to describe *a general* or *an emperor returning home from a grand victory in the enemy's territory.* Specifically, the word "triumph" was used to describe the emperor's triumphal parade when he returned home.

When a returning emperor or general came striding through the gates on his big, powerful, and beautiful horse, he was accompanied by his fellow victorious warriors, who also appeared glorious after their triumphant battle. As the parade followed, the weaponry and treasures seized from the enemy's territory were grandly displayed for all to see.

The grand finale to this triumphal procession was the foreign ruler himself. This ruler had been beaten and bound in chains and was now being forced to walk in disgrace, shame, dishonor, embarrassment, and humiliation as crowds of people came to celebrate his defeat and to get a "peek" at a once-powerful but now totally defeated opponent.

So when Colossians 2:15 declares that Jesus triumphed over evil powers, it is explicitly declaring that Jesus took the enemy apart piece by piece as He thoroughly "spoiled principalities and powers." *When Jesus was finished with those demonic forces, they were utterly plundered — "stripped to bare nakedness" and left with nothing in hand to retaliate!*

Because of the words *parresia* and *triumbeuo,* Colossians 2:15 conveys this idea:

"...He gallantly strode into Heaven to celebrate His victory and the defeat of Satan and his forces. As part of His triumphal process, He flaunted the spoils seized from the hand of the enemy. Yet the greatest spectacle of all occurred when the enemy himself was openly put on display as bound, disgraced, disabled, defeated, humiliated, and stripped bare...."

Jesus' victory over Satan was a momentous affair! When Jesus returned, He was totally triumphant! The party Heaven threw that day was enormous! All of

Heaven's hosts came to celebrate Jesus' victory and Satan's downfall and demise! Right there in front of everyone, Jesus displayed the devil and his cohorts, so all could know that this enemy no longer had the legitimate right or the necessary arms to prolong his rule of terrorism.

Once again, Satan is not a force we are *trying* to defeat; he is *already* defeated. But because very few believers know how to effectively use their God-given authority to resist Satan, he tries to continue illegally operating and doing damage to the souls of men and even to the creation itself.

No matter what demonic strategy may come against you this day or how many demons are assembled together for your destruction, you never have to go down defeated. Jesus *plundered* the enemy when He rose from the dead. So when you look into the mirror, you need to learn to see yourself as one who *already* has the victory. You *already* possess the authority necessary to keep Satan under your feet where he belongs. Remember, you are no longer a victim — *you are a victor!*

My Prayer for Today

Lord, I thank You for the victory You obtained by Your resurrection from the dead! No one else could have done what You did for us. You invaded hell; broke the power of its demonic forces; seized their artillery; and bound the devil. And because You did all this, You set us free! You are our Great Victor, our Great Champion, and You are the Lord of all lords. Thank You for cleansing me with Your blood and granting me the honor to be called a child of God and a joint heir with You. I pray this in Jesus' name!

My Confession for Today

I confess that Satan is not a force I am trying to defeat because he is already defeated. I use my God-given authority to resist him, and he flees from me. No matter what demonic strategy may come against me this day or how many demons may try to assemble together for my destruction, I NEVER have to go down in defeat. When I look into the mirror, I see someone who already has the victory. I possess the authority necessary to keep Satan under my feet where he belongs! I declare this by faith in Jesus' name!

Questions for You to Consider

1. Do you approach life like you are a victorious champion, or a struggling victim?

   _____

   _____

   _____

   _____

   _____

   _____

2. Do you quickly give in to defeat, or do you dig in your heels and refuse to go down defeated?

   _____

   _____

   _____

   _____

   _____

   _____

3. What changes could you make in your thoughts, words, and attitudes to help you maintain a more victorious approach to life?

_____

_____

_____

_____

_____

_____

Day 5

Effective Spiritual Weapons Require Effective Spiritual Strategies

> *For the weapons of our warfare are not carnal, but mighty through God to the pulling down of strong holds.*
>
> — 2 Corinthians 10:4

In this powerful verse, Paul speaks to us about the subject of spiritual warfare. In fact, this is one of the foundational verses on this subject, so it is vital to understand what Paul is talking about. Today I want to especially draw your attention to three words in this power-packed scripture. Pay special attention to the words *weapons, warfare,* and *carnal.*

First, Paul tells us that we have "weapons." These spiritual armaments have been provided by God and are at our disposal. They are both offensive and defensive weapons and can be found in Ephesians 6:13-18, where Paul lists them one by one and explains what each piece represents.

Second, Paul uses the word "warfare." The word "warfare" is taken from the word *stratos.* By choosing to use this word, the Holy Spirit alerts us to some very important facts about spiritual warfare.

The word *stratos* is where we derive the word *strategy.* This informs us that spiritual warfare does not occur accidentally but is something that is *strategically planned.* Just as any army plans its line of attack before a battle begins, the devil plans a line of attack, decides which methods he will use, and chooses the approach he wants to take as he cautiously charts a well-thought-out assault.

But the word *stratos* doesn't just describe the devil's strategies. It also tells us that if we will listen to the Holy Spirit, He will give us a strategy that is superior to any schemes of the devil. The devil is not the only one with a strategy. The Holy Spirit always holds the key to every victory, and He wants to provide us with a divinely-inspired strategy that will render null and void the works of the devil every time!

The Old Testament is filled with examples of divinely-inspired strategies. Consider the case of Joshua and the children of Israel as they stood before the walls of Jericho (Joshua 6:1-27). What strategy did the Lord give them? They were to walk around the walls of Jericho once a day for six days and seven times on the seventh day. Then after the seventh time around the wall on the last day, they were to blow trumpets made of rams' horns. None of this sounded "reasonable" to the natural mind, but the effects of that God-given strategy are still renowned today!

Or consider the time Jehoshaphat sent out a praise team before the army to sing and to worship the Lord (2 Chronicles 20:20-25). What army would send singers and musicians to the frontlines of battle in front of its armed soldiers?

Yet as they sang praises to God and played their instruments, the Lord supernaturally set ambushments and the enemies were smitten.

That day the children of Israel walked away from the battle without losing a single fighter. Not only that, but they were also weighed down with gold, silver, jewels, and other riches in abundance! There was so much plunder that it took them three days to gather it! How did they win this famous battle? They received a strategy from the Lord and then followed it accurately. The results of that strategy are legendary.

In both of these cases, the line of attack made no sense to the natural mind, but it released so much power that it completely crushed the foe. So don't be surprised if the Holy Spirit gives you a strategy that doesn't make sense when you first hear it! Remember, He operates on a higher level than you, and He knows what you don't know. Therefore, He may tell you to do something that seems odd to you at first. But you can be sure that Spirit-inspired strategies always work!

Imagine an army that is fully equipped with weapons of warfare but has no strategy about how to use those weapons against the enemy. Even with all those weapons and artillery at their disposal, an army in this condition would utterly fail.

Likewise, although it's crucial that you put on the whole armor of God, that's just the first step. You must then have a strategy on how to use those weapons and how to attack! Until you receive a strategy from the Lord on how to use your spiritual weapons, they will be of little help in driving back the forces of hell that have come against you.

This leads to the word "carnal." In Greek, this word is *sarkos*, which describes *anything that is of the flesh, fleshly made, or fleshly conjured up* or *anything that is natural or of an unspiritual nature.* Paul uses this word when he writes, "For the weapons of our warfare are not carnal...."

In effect, Paul is saying, *"Don't look to your flesh for the weapons or strategies I'm describing to you because they do not arise out of natural talent, mental exercises, or human efforts. These are spiritual weapons and spiritual strategies, and they come from the spiritual realm."*

When you put all these Greek words together, Second Corinthians 10:4 carries this idea:

"Our God-given weapons are to be used in connection with a divine strategy. But don't look to the flesh to find that strategy, for the battle plan you need is not going to arise out of your own natural talent, mental exercises, or human effort."

If you want to receive the strategy needed to assure your victory, you must turn your attention to the *realm of the Spirit,* for it is from this realm that you will hear from God. You must spend time praying in the Spirit and reading the Word. By yourself, you will never conceive a plan that will deliver you.

Just as spiritual weapons come from God, so do spiritual strategies. So use your head as much as you can, and think through every step. But as you seek God, stay open for Him to graciously give you a supernatural strategy for destroying the work of the devil. And don't be surprised if God tells you to do something that seems a little odd. Since the beginning of time, God has been giving effective strategies that seem strange to the mind of man!

My Prayer for Today

Lord, I know that today I'm going to need a supernatural strategy to do what I need to do. My own natural mind is working all the time to come up with solutions. I'm doing the best I can do, but now I need extra help. I need a divine strategy — a divine idea so powerful and effective that no force will be able to resist it! I know that these kinds of strategies are imparted by the Holy Spirit, so right now I open my heart wide to Him. Holy Spirit, I ask You to drop a supernatural idea into my spirit and soul. Please help me to properly discern it, understand it, and then follow through with obedience. I pray this in Jesus' name!

My Confession for Today

I declare by faith that the Holy Spirit gives me the strategies and ideas I need. I am willing and ready to do whatever He tells me to do. The Spirit of God was sent into this world to be my Helper and my Guide, and I know I can fully rely on Him. I must have His direction, or I won't know what to do. So today He will speak to my heart; I will perceive what He tells me to do; and then I will obediently carry out His good plan for me! I declare this by faith in Jesus' name!

Questions for You to Consider

1. Has the Holy Spirit ever told you to do something that seemed odd to your natural mind but resulted in His power being mightily demonstrated in a situation?

   _____

   _____

   _____

   _____

   _____

2. Have you found that your natural talent, mental reasonings, and human effort are helpless to win the battles you are facing today?

   _____

   _____

   _____

   _____

   _____

3. God is ready to give you the battle plan you need to have victory in your life. Are you willing to spend the time in prayer that is required for you to receive that plan?

_____

_____

_____

_____

_____

_____

Day 6

Why Should We Stop Just Because the Devil Gets in the Way?

> *Wherefore we would have come unto you, even I Paul, once and again; but Satan hindered us.*
>
> — 1 Thessalonians 2:18

I f you are going to do anything significant for the Kingdom of God, you must know in advance that Satan will not be delighted about it. He will try to stop you, thwart you, and dissuade you from staying on track. The last thing he wants is for you to step into the middle of God's will for your life, because he knows the moment you do, mighty and powerful things will begin to happen that negatively affect his dark kingdom. Therefore, Satan will most definitely do all he can to keep you from getting where God wants you to be!

In First Thessalonians 2:18, Paul gives his own testimony of how Satan tried to hinder him from doing what God put in his heart. He wrote, "Wherefore we would have come unto you, even I Paul, once and again; but Satan hindered us."

The word "hindered" is the Greek word *egkopto* and was used to *depict a runner who was elbowed out of the race by a fellow runner.* However, it was also used to picture *the breaking up of a road to make it impassable for travelers.* This kind of *impasse* made it impossible for a traveler to get where he needed to go. As a result, the traveler's trip was *hindered, delayed, postponed,* or *temporarily put off.* The traveler could still take another route to get to the same destination, but the alternate route was inconvenient, cost a lot of extra money, and took precious time that could have been used another way.

By using this word, Paul informs us that demonic attacks inconvenienced him on occasion. Satan craftily sought to abort advances of the Gospel by arranging unexpected problems that delayed, postponed, and hindered the missions God had placed on Paul's heart. But did Paul sit down and cry because plans didn't work out as he intended? Did he throw in the towel and quit? *No!*

The apostle Paul never stopped just because the devil tried to get in his way! No impasse or roadblock was going to stop him! He refused to take no for an answer! He was going to get the job done, regardless of the inconvenience, money, time, or effort involved. He was so stubborn about doing what he was called to do that he always found a way to do it.

An example of this is the time Paul left the city of Ephesus because his life was in danger (*see* Acts 19 and 20). Paul had given three years of his life to the believers in Ephesus. When he left, he could have cried, "Oh, I don't understand why the Lord let this happen! He knows how much I love the leadership of Ephesus!" Paul could have bemoaned, "Now I'll never see the Ephesian believers again. The devil has attacked me, and the door to Ephesus is permanently closed for me!"

But Paul understood that crying and lamenting don't change a thing. So instead, he went down the road to the seaside town of Miletus and secured a facility for a meeting. Then he called for the elders of Ephesus to meet him there! Paul figured if he couldn't go to Ephesus, why not invite the leadership to come see him? Why resign himself to defeat just because he had hit an impasse in the road? Paul knew that there is more than one way to accomplish a goal. So he put his brain to work and found a way to do what God wanted him to do.

Why should we stop just because the devil gets in the way? If that were the case, we might as well stop everything we're doing for the Lord right now! There will never be a time that the devil just lets us do what is in our hearts. We must be determined to keep doing what we're called to do even if the devil tries to slam the door shut in our faces.

So what if Satan shut the door to Ephesus? That was a good time for Paul to look for an open window! If he couldn't go to the elders, why not call them to him? Paul discovered an open window in Miletus. He called for the leaders, met with them, and finished his assignment, exactly as God had ordered him to do. *Mission accomplished!*

You see, Paul had an attitude that would not give up. It didn't matter how much opposition was leveled against him, he had already decided he would out-live the opposition. Somehow he'd find a way to do what God had called him to do.

You can do anything God calls you to do too! Determine in your heart that you will not allow Satan to do anything to stop you, thwart you, or dissuade you from staying on track with the assignment God has given you. God's will for your life is where mighty and powerful things are going to happen! That is why the devil is putting up such a fuss to try to keep you from getting there. He's afraid of what will happen if you actually do what God has put in your heart to do.

So dig in your heels, and determine that you are not giving in or giving up. Refuse to back up or relent, and keep on pressing ahead. The devil may have put an impasse in the road before you, but that doesn't mean the show is over! If you'll listen to the Holy Spirit, He'll show you another route to get you where you need to be.

The Holy Spirit needs a partner who is committed. So just commit yourself to pressing ahead, regardless of the opposition. As you do, the Spirit of God will empower you to conquer every attack that comes against you. Then He will masterfully show you another and more effective way to fulfill your divine assignment. *In the end, the devil will be sorry he messed with you!*

My Prayer for Today

Lord, I ask You to help me stay fiercely committed to fulfilling the assignment You have given to me. Forgive me for the times I've given in to weakness and allowed myself to complain when I should have grabbed hold of Your strength and pressed full steam ahead. I repent for allowing my flesh to talk me into moments of defeat. Today I choose to push forward to do exactly what You've told me to do. Holy Spirit, if the devil creates an impasse for me, please show me a better route to take so I can fulfill my divine assignment! I pray this in Jesus' name!

My Confession for Today

I confess that I am led by the Holy Spirit and that He shows me how to get around every obstacle the devil tries to put in my path. No impasse the devil puts before me is sufficient to prevent me from achieving what Jesus has asked me to do and to be. I refuse to accept no for an answer, and I reject any temptation to quit. I am empowered by the Spirit of the Almighty God, and I can do anything He will ever ask me to do! I declare this by faith in Jesus' name!

Questions for You to Consider

1. Has there been a time in your life when it seemed like an impasse stood between you and what God wanted you to do? How did you respond to that impasse?

_____

_____

_____

_____

_____

_____

2. If you listened to the Holy Spirit and found another, better route to finish the task before you, did it thrill your heart to realize that He knows how to get around every attack of the enemy? What did you learn by following the Holy Spirit rather than allowing discouragement to hold you back from fulfilling your divine assignment?

_____

_____

_____

_____

_____

_____

3. Who are the people in your life who seem blocked from doing what God wants them to do? Could you be an encouragement to these individuals by contacting them and sharing how God supernaturally led you around impasses in the past?

_____

_____

_____

_____

_____

_____

Day 7

Take Up Your Shield of Faith!

> *Above all, taking the shield of faith, wherewith ye shall be able to quench all the fiery darts of the wicked.*
>
> — Ephesians 6:16

Many people wrongly assume that the shield of faith is the most important part of their spiritual weaponry because Paul said, *"Above all,* taking the shield of faith..." (Ephesians 6:16). But if you think about it for a moment, you see that the shield of faith *can't* be more important than the "loinbelt of truth" — the Word of God — because faith comes from God's Word (Romans 10:17).

So just what *did* Paul mean when he said, "Above all...."? The phrase "above all" is taken from the Greek phrase *epi pasin.* The word *epi* means over. The word *pasin* means *all* or *everything.* So rather than stating that the shield of faith is more important than the other pieces of armor, the phrase *epi pasin* describes the *position* faith should have over the other pieces of armor. It could be better translated, *"Out in front of all...."* or *"Covering all...."*

Therefore, the phrase "above all" emphatically tells you that your "shield of faith" is never meant to be held next to your side or timidly held behind your back. Faith is supposed to be *out front* where it can *completely cover* you and protect you from harm — especially when you are marching forward to take new ground for the Kingdom of God!

Just as Roman soldiers kept their shields out in front of them to defend them from deadly attacks and blows from their enemies, God wants you to tightly grip your shield of faith while keeping it out in front where it can protect and defend you. When your shield of faith is kept in this *out-front* and *covering* position, it can do what God intended for it to do! This is why Paul continues to say, "...wherewith ye shall be able to quench all the fiery darts of the wicked."

But it is also very important for you to notice that Paul says, *"...Taking* the shield of faith...." The word "taking" is from the word *analambano,* which is a compound of the Greek words *ana* and *lambano.* The word ana means *up, back,* or *again;* the word lambano means *to take up* or *to take in hand.* When compounded together, it means *to take something up in hand* or *to pick something back up again.* This plainly means your shield of faith can be either *picked up* or *laid down.* It places the responsibility on you as to whether you will use your shield of faith or allow yourself to go through life unprotected.

If you want to employ the use of your faith, you must make the choice to take it in hand and to place it in front of you. It will not assume its defensive position over your life by accident. Your faith will only operate in your life the way it was meant to do when you choose to pick it up and put it where it belongs — *out in front.*

If you ever go into battle without your shield of faith, you are making a mistake you will seriously regret. Keeping your shield of faith in position is not an option if you intend to overcome the enemy and win the battles that are before you.

Therefore, I urge you not to go into battle without this all-important piece of your spiritual armor. If you fail to keep that protective shield in front of you, you leave yourself exposed to the deadly strikes of your adversary, the devil.

On the other hand, as you choose to daily take up your shield of faith, holding it out in front of you so that it completely covers every part of your life, you put yourself in position to thwart every single attack that the enemy throws your way!

My Prayer for Today

Lord, I thank You for giving me a shield of faith that completely covers me from head to toe. I don't have to constantly succumb to the devil's attacks. By holding my shield of faith above all and out in front so that it covers me completely as You intended it to do, I can be protected from the attacks that the enemy would like to wage against me. Forgive me for the times I've let my shield lay at my side while I stayed busy complaining about the devil giving me fits. I realize now that it's up to me to pick up my shield of faith and put it where it belongs. So with Your help, Lord, I am reaching out right now to pick it up, to hold it out front, and to do my part to make sure the enemy has no access to me! I pray this in Jesus' name!

My Confession for Today

I confess that God has given me a shield of faith that protects me against the works of the enemy. If I will hold my faith out front — and today I commit myself to doing just that — God's Word guarantees that this mighty shield will thwart the fiery darts that the enemy wants so desperately to throw at me. My shield will cause those darts to bounce off, thereby protecting me from being struck. I will walk with my shield of faith out in front so that it covers me as God intended for it to do. As long as I do that, I can be confident that I will move forward in life without the enemy winning any full-scale attack against me! I declare this by faith in Jesus' name!

Questions for You to Consider

1. Can you say that your faith is alive and active and out in front of you as God intended for it to be, or have you allowed your faith to become inactive so that it lags behind?

_____

_____

_____

_____

_____

_____

2. Please answer these questions honestly, for a truthful answer may prevent future disaster in your life: Did you once walk in faith more consistently than you do today? Have you allowed your shield of faith to drop to your side instead of maintaining it in the forward position that allows it to defend you from the enemy's attacks?

_____

_____

_____

_____

_____

_____

3. What steps are you going to take to reignite your faith and return it to its position as the mighty shield of protection that God intended for it to be? What kind of plan are you going to follow to see your faith recharged, reenergized, and repositioned out in front of your life?

_____

_____

_____

_____

_____

_____

Day 8

Are You Wearing Your Killer Shoes?

> *Stand therefore, having your loins girt about with truth, and having on the breastplate of righteousness; and your feet shod with the preparation of the gospel of peace.*
>
> — Ephesians 6:14,15

If you had seen the shoes of a Roman soldier, you'd have wanted to make sure you didn't fall in front of him or get in his way where he might accidentally step on you. Those weren't normal shoes — they were *killer shoes!*

Paul refers to these killer shoes in Ephesians 6:15 as he talks about the spiritual weapons God has given to the Church. Just as God has given each believer a sword, He has also clothed every believer with the shoes of peace.

Now, I realize that these shoes may sound like a passive, peaceful part of our spiritual armor. However, these are actually *killer shoes,* such as those worn by a Roman soldier.

The shoes of a Roman soldier were *vicious weapons.* They began at the top of the legs near the knees and extended down to the feet. The portions that covered the knees to the feet were called the "greaves." They were made of metal and were specially shaped to wrap around the calves of a soldier's legs. The greaves were uncomfortable but essential for the safekeeping of a soldier's legs.

The shoe itself was made of heavy pieces of leather or metal, tied together with leather straps that were intermingled with bits of metal. The bottoms were manufactured of heavy leather or pieces of metal. The bottom of the shoes were affixed with sharp, dangerous, protruding spikes. These spikes had several purposes, which we will get to in just a moment. In addition, two sharply pointed spikes extended beyond the front of each shoe.

Let me explain to you the reasons for all this gear on a soldier's legs and feet. First, the greaves — the metal that covered the Roman soldier's legs from his knees to the top of his feet — were designed to protect the soldier's calves when he was required to march through rocky and thorny terrain. If he'd had no protection on his legs, he would have surely been gashed and cut by the environment.

Thus, the greaves gave the soldier protection so he could keep walking, regardless of the obstacles he encountered. The metal barriers also gave him defensive protection in those moments when an adversary kicked him in the shins, trying to break his legs. Because the soldier's calves were covered with these greaves, his legs could not be broken and the enemy's attacks were in vain.

Now let's talk about the spikes on the bottom of the soldier's shoes. These were intended to hold him "in place" when in battle. His opponent might try to push him around, but the spikes on the bottom of his shoes helped keep him in his place, making the soldier virtually immovable. Additionally, those spikes on the bottom and front of the shoes served as weapons of brutality and murder. One good kick with those shoes, and an enemy would be dead. Just a few seconds of stomping on a fallen adversary would have eradicated that foe forever!

When Paul writes about these shoes in Ephesians 6:15, he says, "...And your feet shod with the preparation of the gospel of peace." Notice that he connects *peace* with these killer weapons! In just a moment, you'll understand why.

The word "shod" is derived from the word *hupodeomai* — a compound of the words *hupo* and *deo*. The word *hupo* means *under,* and *deo* means *to bind.* Taken together as one word, it conveys the idea of *binding something very tightly on the bottom of one's feet.* Therefore, this is not the picture of a loosely fitting shoe but of a shoe that has been tied onto the bottom of the foot *extremely tightly.*

Just as the greaves of a Roman soldier protected him from the environment and from the blows of his enemy, the peace of God — when it is operating in your life — protects and defends you from the hassles and assaults of the devil. The enemy may try to disrupt you, distract you, and steal your attention by causing negative events to whirl all around you, but his attempts will fail because the peace of God, like a protective greave, stops you from being hurt and enables you to keep marching forward!

Just as those spikes held a Roman soldier securely in place when his enemy tried to push him around, the peace of God will hold you in place when the devil tries to push you around! And as the soldier used those spikes to kick and to kill his opponent, there is no need for you to ever stop moving ahead just because the devil tries to block your path. If he is foolish enough to try to get in front of you, just keep walking! Stomp all along the way! By the time you're finished using your shoes of peace, you won't have much of a devil problem to deal with anymore!

Paul uses this illustration to tell us that we must firmly tie God's peace onto our lives. If we only give peace a loosely fitting position in our lives, it won't be long before the affairs of life knock our peace out of place. Hence, we must bind peace onto our minds and emotions in the same way Roman soldiers made sure to *bind* their shoes very tightly onto their feet.

But wait — there's one more important point. Paul continued, "And your feet shod with *the preparation....*" The word "preparation" is the Greek word *etoimasin,* and it presents the idea of *readiness* or *preparation.* When used in connection with Roman soldiers, the word *etoimasin* portrayed *men of war who had their shoes tied on very tightly to ensure a firm footing.* Once they had the assurance that their shoes were going to stay in place, they were ready to march out onto the battlefield and confront the enemy.

When peace is in place in your life, it gives you the assurance you need to step out in faith and make the moves God is leading you to make. But before you take those steps, you need to be sure His peace is operating in your life. This mighty and powerful piece of your spiritual weaponry is essential because, without it, the devil can try to kick, punch, pull, and distract you. But with that conquering peace firmly tied to your mind and emotions, you will be empowered to keep marching ahead, impervious to the devil's attempts to take you down!

My Prayer for Today

Lord, I thank You for the peace You have placed in my life. This powerful spiritual weapon protects me from the assaults of life, enabling me to stand fixed, even in the face of the occasional storms that try to blow into my life, my family, my church, my friendships, and my business. How can I ever express how much I need this peace or how grateful I am to You for covering me with this protective shield that fortifies me and makes me strong? When adverse situations arise against me, help me remember to immediately release this divine force to safeguard my life. I pray this in Jesus' name!

My Confession for Today

I confess that God's peace rules my mind and emotions, protecting me from the ups and downs of life. When storms are trying to rage against me and situations are hostile toward me, God's peace covers and safeguards me from all harm. Because divine peace is operating in me, I am not easily moved, quickly shaken, or terrified by any events that occur around about me. This mighty and powerful piece of spiritual weaponry is mine to use day and night. Therefore, although the devil may try to kick, punch, pull, and distract me, that conquering peace empowers me to keep marching ahead, oblivious to the devil's attempts to take me down! I declare this by faith in Jesus' name!

Questions for You to Consider

1. Have there been some very difficult times in your life when the peace of God protected you from the turmoil that was happening around you?

_____

_____

_____

_____

_____

_____

2. Do you recall how you felt when you were enveloped in this supernatural peace? Think about it.

_____

_____

_____

_____

_____

_____

3. If the devil is trying to shove you around emotionally right now, what can you do to stay in the peace of God?

_____

_____

_____

_____

_____

_____

Day 9

Here's How To Extinguish the Fiery Darts of the Wicked!

> *Above all, taking the shield of faith, wherewith ye shall be able to quench all the fiery darts of the wicked.*
>
> — Ephesians 6:16

Would you like to extinguish every flaming dart the devil ever tries to shoot in your direction? Does that proposal sound too good to be true? Well, Ephesians 6:16 assures you that if you have your shield of faith lifted high in front of you, you will be supernaturally empowered to defend yourself against the fiery darts of the enemy. But more than that, you will be able to literally *extinguish* every single fiery dart the devil will ever try to send your way!

This makes our shield of faith very important! Therefore, let's look at Ephesians 6:16 to see exactly what it says about us being able to extinguish all the flaming arrows of the enemy. It says, "Above all, taking the shield of faith, wherewith ye shall be able to quench all the fiery darts of the wicked."

Today I would like to draw your attention to several very important points in this verse. First, I want you to notice the phrase "...wherewith ye shall be able...." The first part of this Greek phrase would be better translated *by which*. For the words "ye shall be able," the Greek word used here is the word *dunamis*, which denotes *explosive power* or *dynamic power* and is where we get the word "dynamite." When these Greek words and phrases are used together as they are in Ephesians 6:16, it could actually be translated, *"Above all, taking the shield of faith, by which you will be dynamically empowered...."*

Paul uses these Greek words to explain the supernatural empowerment that occurs when a believer uses his shield of faith. When a believer lifts his shield high and holds it out in front of him where it belongs, that shield divinely energizes the believer to stand bravely against every assault of the devil. That shield of faith becomes dynamically and supernaturally empowered to act as an impenetrable wall of defense against the enemy's tactics. *In other words, faith is a shield to the believer!*

The shield of faith is so powerful that it makes you fortified, invulnerable, and armed to the teeth! It equips you to hold an ironclad position. It turns you into a spiritual tank so you have the ability to move your position forward without taking any losses yourself. This doesn't mean the devil won't try to stop you, but when the shield of faith is held out in front of you as it ought to be, you become divinely empowered "...to quench all the fiery darts of the wicked."

The word "quench" in this verse is the Greek word *sbennumi,* which means *to quench by dousing* or *to extinguish by drowning in water*. It refers to the water-soaked shield of Roman soldiers. You see, before Roman soldiers went out to battle, they purposely soaked their shields in water until they were completely water-saturated. The soldiers did this because they knew the enemy would be shooting firebearing arrows in their direction. If a shield was dry, it was possible for it to be set on fire when struck. But if this vital piece of armor was water-soaked, the flames would be extinguished even if an arrow penetrated its heavily saturated surface.

How does this apply to us as believers? Well, Romans 10:17 says that our faith is increased by hearing the Word of God. In Ephesians 5:26, the Word of God is likened to water. So as we regularly submit ourselves to the Word of God, we soak our faith with the Word just as a Roman soldier soaked his shield with water. And when our faith becomes Word-saturated or Word-soaked, it becomes just like the soldier's water-saturated shield. In other words, it will be so heavily inundated with the water of God's Word that even if a fiery dart pierces our shield, the huge amount of Word in us will extinguish the flames and put out a potentially damaging situation!

The words "fiery darts" are from the Greek word *belos*. It referred to *an arrow with its tip wrapped with fabric soaked in flammable fluids so it would burn with hot and angry flames*. The famous Greek writer Thycidides used this Greek word *belos* to depict specially-made, long, slender arrows that outwardly looked harmless; however, the hollow interior of the arrow was filled with flammable fluids that, upon impact, exploded into a raging fire. This last arrow is most likely the picture that Paul had in his mind when he wrote about the "...fiery darts of the wicked."

Often when the devil strikes, his attack looks inconsequential at first, like harmless little arrows that can do little damage. But when those arrows strike into the heart or emotions, they often explode and set human passions aflame, causing a minor issue to develop into a fierce, flaming situation. The damage done in such a moment is very serious — and all of it could have been avoided if the shield of faith had been held high and regularly doused in the water of the Word!

There is no doubt that the devil will try to shoot his arrows in your direction. But having a shield of faith that is soaked in the Word of God gives you double protection against these attacks. It guarantees that the enemy's fiery darts will have little or no effect, even if they get close enough to strike your heart, mind, or emotions in the midst of the situations you find yourself facing today.

So I urge you today to take the time to soak your faith in the Word of God. Let the water of the Word so saturate your faith that if the enemy tries to launch a surprise attack on you — your health, your finances, your marriage, your children, your family, your church, your business, or your job — he will find that his fiery darts have no impact on your Word-soaked faith shield!

Refuse to let yourself become the devil's victim! Hold your Word-doused shield of faith high in front of you so it completely covers your life. Then rest assured that no fiery dart of the enemy will make any serious impact on you. *That faith shield will protect you from anything the enemy throws at you through the dynamic, explosive power of God!*

My Prayer for Today

Lord, thank You for giving me the shield of faith. Help me to be brave and bold and to hold my shield high in front of me to stop every attack of the enemy. After reading today's Sparkling Gem, I understand that I have a responsibility to soak my faith in Your Word so it can extinguish each and every flaming arrow the devil tries to shoot into my life. I ask You to help me be sincerely committed to making Your Word the top priority in my life — soaking my faith with that Word until it becomes an impenetrable wall of defense against the enemy's attacks! I pray this in Jesus' name!

My Confession for Today

I confess that my faith is saturated with the Word of God! The devil may try to attack me, but my faith is held out high in front of me, covering my life completely and extinguishing every flaming arrow the devil attempts to shoot in my direction. My faith is supernaturally energized, and I am empowered to stand against every assault the devil tries to make on my life! I declare this by faith in Jesus' name!

Questions for You to Consider

1. Are you spending enough time in the Word to see that your shield of faith is soaked and saturated with the water of God's Word? Or is your faith so parched from a lack of the Word that your shield isn't working anymore?

_____

_____

_____

_____

_____

2. Can you remember a time when a fiery dart struck that would have normally set everything ablaze with negative emotions and destruction — but because your faith was Word-soaked and in place, that attack had very little impact in your life? What was that situation?

_____

_____

_____

_____

_____

3. Have you ever seen a fiery dart from the enemy that released a blaze of destruction when it struck? When you saw it happen, did you realize that the success of the devil's attack was due to a lack of time in God's Word?

_____

_____

_____

_____

_____

_____

Day 10

A Unique Receptacle Specially Made for the Power of God!

> *Finally, my brethren, be strong in the Lord, and in the power of his might.*
>
> — Ephesians 6:10

Could you use some extra strength today? I want to draw your attention to the word "strong" in Ephesians 6:10. It is the Greek word *endunamao*, a compound of the words *en* and *dunamis*. The word *en* means *in*. The word *dunamis* means *explosive strength, ability,* and *power*. It's where we get the word *dynamite*.

Thus, this word *endunamao* presents the picture of *an explosive power that is being deposited into some type of container, vessel, or other form of receptacle*. The very nature of this word *endunamao* means that there necessarily must be some type of receiver for this power to be deposited *into*.

This is where we come into the picture! We are specially designed by God to be the receptacles of divine power. When Paul tells us to be strong in the Lord, he is essentially saying, "Receive a supernatural, strengthening, internal deposit of power into your inner man." God is the Giver, and we are the *receptacles* into which this power is to be deposited.

Paul knew you and I would desperately need supernatural power in order to successfully combat the attacks the enemy would bring against us. That's why he urges us to open our spirits, souls, and bodies to God so we can receive this supernatural strength.

Ephesians 6:10 could be translated to mean:

"...Be infused with supernatural strength and ability...."

"...Be empowered with this special touch of God's strength...."

"...Receive this inner strengthening...."

God wants you and me to have this supernatural strength and ability! We are the special receptacles or containers He created to possess this phenomenal power. Think of how wonderful it is that God specially fashioned you and me to be the containers for the power of God!

So if you're feeling a need for extra strength today, open your heart right now and allow God to give you a fresh infilling of His explosive, Holy Spirit power!

My Prayer for Today

Lord, it is clear that You want me to be filled with Your power and strength today, so I open my heart right now and ask You to fill me with Your Spirit. Thank You for creating me to be the receptacle for this wonderful power — and by faith, I receive a fresh infilling of Your Spirit right now! I pray this in Jesus' name!

My Confession for Today

I declare by faith that I am filled with the Spirit of God. I am specially made by God to be the container of the Holy Spirit. He lives in me; He fills me; and He empowers me to conquer every attack that the devil tries to bring against me. God knew I needed this power and therefore gave it to me. I boldly confess that I am FILLED with the supernatural, wonder-working, and dynamic power of the Holy Spirit! I declare this by faith in Jesus' name!

Questions for You to Consider

1. Do you feel a need for more strength and power in your life today?

_____

_____

_____

_____

_____

_____

2. Have you asked the Lord to refill you with the power of the Holy Spirit? Why don't you take a few minutes right now to open your heart and let the Lord fill you with a new surge of divine power?

_____

_____

_____

_____

_____

_____

3. What steps can you take today to avail yourself to a special touch of the Holy Spirit's strength?

_____

_____

_____

_____

_____

_____

Day 11

Preparing the Troops for Battle!

> *Not forsaking the assembling of ourselves together, as the manner of some is; but exhorting one another....*
>
> — Hebrews 10:25

The word "exhorting" is a powerful little word! It's the Greek word *parakaleo,* a compound of the words *para* and *kaleo. Para* means *alongside* and *kaleo* means *to call, to beckon,* or *to speak to someone.* When these two words are compounded together, it depicts *someone who is right alongside of a person, urging him, beseeching him, begging him to make some kind of correct decision.*

In the ancient Greek world, this word was often used by military leaders before they sent their troops into battle. Rather than hide from the painful reality of war, the leaders would summon their troops together and speak straightforwardly with them about the potential dangers of the battlefield. The leaders would also tell their troops about the glories of winning a major victory.

Rather than ignore the clear-cut dangers of battle, these officers came right alongside their troops and urged, exhorted, beseeched, begged, and pleaded with them *to stand tall; throw their shoulders back; look the enemy straight on, eyeball to eyeball; and face their battles bravely.*

Walking by faith and doing the will of God sometimes places us in the midst of spiritual battles. Sometimes these battles aren't won quickly.

If you know someone who is discouraged because his fight isn't won yet, speak to that person truthfully and in a straightforward manner the way a commanding officer would speak to his troops. Remind the person of others who have stood the test of time and won their battles. And be sure to remind him of the sweetness of victory when the battle is over. He needs to hear a passionate, heartfelt word of exhortation from you!

The word "exhort" in Hebrews 10:25 could mean:

"When you're feeling down and out — like a failure who is falling behind everyone else — that isn't the time for you to stay away from other believers, as some are in the habit of doing. That is the very time that you need to come together for the sake of encouragement so you can face your battles more bravely...."

Do you know people who need some encouragement today? Instead of letting the day slip by before you know it, why not take the time *right now* to call those individuals and encourage them? If you can't call them, how about *writing them a note* that will help them focus on victory?

Think back to all those moments in your own life when someone came alongside of you to encourage you. Didn't it make a big difference in your life? Now it's your turn to return this blessing to someone else.

So determine today to be a real comrade in the Lord to another Christian soldier. Make it your aim to speak words of encouragement to those around you today. *If you see someone who is discouraged, or if you know someone who has been struggling in his or her faith, go out of your way to encourage the troops!*

My Prayer for Today

Lord, today I want to be used by You to encourage someone! I ask You to lead me to those You want me to encourage. Show me what to say, how much to say, and when to say it. Teach me to recognize the needs in other people and not to focus only on my own needs. I pray this in Jesus' name!

My Confession for Today

I confess that I am going to be a major blessing in someone's life today. The Holy Spirit is going to open my eyes and show me exactly whom I am supposed to encourage. With the help of the Spirit, I will speak the right words at the right time, and I will say only as much as I need to say. When this day concludes, someone will thank God for the way I stepped into his or her life to be a source of encouragement! I declare this by faith in Jesus' name!

Questions for You to Consider

1. Have you been so focused on your own challenges that you've failed to recognize the needs of others who are around you?

_____

_____

_____

_____

_____

_____

2. Can you think of some people in your life who need encouragement and extra strength today?

_____

_____

_____

_____

_____

_____

3. Can you make a list of practical ways you can reach out to encourage these individuals and let them know you are thinking of them today?

_____

_____

_____

_____

_____

_____

Day 12

What Should You Do When Your Plans Seem Hindered?

> *Wherefore we would have come unto you, even I Paul, once and again; but Satan hindered us.*
>
> — 1 Thessalonians 2:18

Have you ever pursued something that you believed was God's will, yet obstacles seemed to keep you from doing what you thought you were supposed to do? If you have, don't feel alone, because many people have been in that same position! Even the apostle Paul felt this way from time to time! *But what should you do in times like these?*

Today I want you to particularly notice the word "hindered" in the verse above. It comes from the Greek word *egkopto*, an old word that was originally used to describe *a road so deteriorated and broken up that it was impassable.*

Have you ever driven down a road on your way to your destination, only to discover that the road you're driving on is too full of ruts and holes to continue your journey? As a result, you have to turn around, go back, and find another route to get where you are going. Well, that is exactly the image the word *egkopto* portrays to us!

Paul uses this word to describe hindering forces that kept him from going to see the Thessalonians. There is no doubt that this means Paul was on his way to see them — not once, he says, but twice. But the journey became so filled with danger and unexpected bumps that Paul had to turn around, go back, and rethink his strategy on how he was going to get to the church at Thessalonica. Can you think of a time when you encountered something like this in your own journey?

But the word *egkopto* means even more than this! It was also used in Greek times in an *athletic* sense. It was used to portray the moment when *a runner comes alongside another runner and literally elbows him out of the race.* Although the second runner was running a good race, *he is shoved out of the way by the aggression* of his fellow runner. As a result of this action, the runner who was elbowed loses the leading edge he previously held.

This categorically means that Paul understood Satan's tactics. The enemy had tried to make use of dangerous and unexpected bumps along the way to throw Paul off track and to elbow him out of his spiritual race. In fact, Paul was convinced that Satan had specifically engineered these unforeseen and unanticipated hassles to keep him from getting to the Thessalonian church.

When these two ideas are combined together, the primary idea of the word "hindered" becomes that of *an impasse so severe that it prohibits you from going where you need to go or an aggressor who unkindly elbows you off course in your spiritual race.*

Paul is actually saying:

"...Satan created an impasse that kept me from coming to see you."

"...Satan put obstructions in my path to prevent me from getting to you."

"...Satan cut in on me and prohibited me from visiting you as I wanted to do."

"...Satan tried to elbow his way in on me to keep me from coming to see you."

When something happens that seems to prohibit you from doing the will of God, remember that you are not the first to encounter such difficulties. Others have been in the same quandary. In time, however, the devil's attack ceased, and the way for them to move ahead became clear. In the same way, you can be sure that God is going to empower you and give you the wisdom you need to get where you need to go!

Don't despair — the story isn't over yet! Don't throw in the towel and give in just because you've hit some kind of impasse. The devil has never had the last word on anything, and he isn't going to have the last word on this situation either. *Regardless of what the devil has tried to do, it's time for you to remember that what God promised SHALL come to pass as you hold fast to your faith in Him!*

My Prayer for Today

Lord, I've run into an impasse, and I don't know how to get past it by myself. I have done everything I know to do, but the problem continues to persist in my life. Today I am asking You for the strength I need to keep pushing forward and to overcome the obstacles that Satan has set in my path. I know that greater is He who is in me than he that is in the world, so today I fervently ask that the power of God residing within me be released to overcome each attack the devil has tried to bring against me. I pray this in Jesus' name!

My Confession for Today

I know I am not the first to encounter difficulties. Therefore, I confess that with God's help, the devil's attack will cease and the way for me to move ahead will become clear. God is going to give me the exact wisdom I need to get where I need to go! I am not going to give in just because I've hit some kind of impasse. The devil has never had the last word on anything, and he isn't going to have the last word on this situation either! I declare this by faith in Jesus' name!

Questions for You to Consider

1. Can you think of times in your life when you've experienced impasses that eventually moved out of the way?

_____

_____

_____

_____

_____

_____

2. What actions did you take that caused those devilish assaults and roadblocks to dissipate?

_____

_____

_____

_____

_____

_____

3. Have you asked the Holy Spirit to show you the real root cause of any current impasse you're facing, as well as the steps you can take to close the door to the devil and reverse your situation?

_____
_____
_____
_____
_____
_____

Day 13

Comrades in the Lord Jesus Christ

> *I charge you by the Lord that this epistle be read unto all the holy brethren.*
>
> — 1 Thessalonians 5:27

Throughout Paul's writings in the New Testament, he uses the word "brethren" when he writes to the churches. This word comes from the Greek word *adelphos,* which is one of the oldest words in the New Testament. In the King James Version, it is usually translated as the word "brethren." However, it actually has a much deeper meaning than this.

In its very oldest sense, the word *adelphos* ("brother") was used by physicians in the medical world to describe *two people who were born from the same womb.* So when the early Greeks addressed each other as "brethren," they meant to convey the idea: *"You and I are brothers! We came out of the same womb of humanity.*

We have the same feelings; we have similar emotions; and we deal with the same problems in life. In every respect, we are truly brothers!"

In part, this was Paul's thinking when he addressed his readers as "brethren." By using this terminology, he brought himself right down to the level of his readers to identify with their position in life and with their personal struggles and victories. They were truly brothers — born from the womb of God, related by the blood of Jesus Christ, and members of the same spiritual family.

But the word "brethren" also had another very significant meaning during New Testament times, a meaning that it doesn't have in our world today. It was used during the time of Alexander the Great to describe faithful *soldiers.* These fighting men were true *brothers, comrades,* and *partners* who were united to fight the same fight, handle the same weapons, and win the same wars!

From time to time, Alexander the Great would hold huge public ceremonies where he would give awards to soldiers who had gone the extra mile in battle. When the most coveted awards were given, Alexander the Great would beckon the most faithful soldiers on stage to stand next to him. Before an audience of adoring soldiers, Alexander would embrace each faithful soldier and publicly declare, "Alexander the Great is proud to be the brother of this soldier!"

That word "brother" was this same Greek word *adelphos,* but in this instance, it referred to military men who were *brothers in battle.* This was the highest and greatest compliment that could be given to a solider during the time of Alexander the Great.

Thus, to be a "brother" meant that a person was a true *comrade.* Through the thick and thin of battle, these soldiers stood together, achieving a special level of brotherhood known only by those who stay united together in the heat of the fray. This was also part of what Paul had in mind when he wrote to the Early Church.

When Paul called his fellow Christians "brothers," he was telling them:

"In addition to being blood brothers, we are all in a similar fight, slugging it out against the same enemy — and this common fight makes us real comrades...."

I'm sure that Paul's readers were probably struggling in their personal lives, just as we do today, but they hadn't given up the fight. They were still on the front lines, slugging it out and plodding along, one step at a time. They were the kind of believers who are worth knowing and worthy to be called brothers because they possessed an ongoing commitment to stay faithful in the battle and committed to the cause.

No matter how well or how badly these believers were doing in the midst of their fight, at least they were *still fighting!* Others had given up, but they had not. As long as they remained faithful to the fight and refused to relinquish their stand of faith, Paul viewed them as exceptionally fine soldiers — the kind of soldiers anyone would be happy to associate with!

The word "brother" emphatically declares that it's not really how well you fight in life that counts. What really counts is that you keep on fighting! So don't give up on yourself, and don't give up on those believers around you who seem to be struggling. As long as they keep on trying — as long as they stay in the battle — they're worthy of your friendship! *You should be proud to be associated with people of such a spiritual caliber!*

My Prayer for Today

Lord, I ask You to help me see myself and other Christian brothers and sisters as soldiers in the army of God. Help me develop an attitude of determination that refuses to surrender to hardship or to throw in the towel in the face of difficulty. At the same time that this attitude is being developed inside me, use me to help fortify the same determined attitude in other Christian soldiers who face hostile forces that have come to steal their victory and joy. I pray this in Jesus' name!

My Confession for Today

I confess that regardless of how much resistance the devil is trying to bring against my life, I will never surrender to defeat. Others may give up, but not me! As long as I am alive, I will stay in the fight. I refuse to relinquish my stand of faith. I am an exceptionally fine soldier — exactly the kind other Christian soldiers should be happy to associate with — because I am committed and determined to fight until my victory is complete! I declare this by faith in Jesus' name!

Questions for You to Consider

1. Can you name five people who have been real "comrades" in your life?

   _____

   _____

   _____

   _____

   _____

   _____

2. In your mind, what qualifies a person to be a bona fide friend?

   _____

   _____

   _____

   _____

   _____

   _____

3. What practical things can you do to become a better friend to those you love, and how can you start this process today?

_____

_____

_____

_____

_____

_____

Day 14

Never Forget That You Are More Than a Conqueror!

> *Nay, in all these things we are more than conquerors through him that loved us.*
>
> — Romans 8:37

How do you see yourself? As a champion who wins nearly every fight? Or as a loser — someone who struggles along, never seeming to conquer a single problem? How you perceive yourself is very important because it will ultimately affect the way other people see you.

Have you ever met someone who had a bad self-image or who always seemed to carry an air of inferiority around with him? It isn't hard to discern this attitude in people. They feel so badly about themselves that they *exude* their negative perception of themselves and their sense of insecurity. On the other hand, if you've ever met individuals who are self-confident and self-assured, you know that it's easy to recognize their confidence. Why? Because a confident person exudes confidence.

It is simply a fact that you will inevitably *project* what you feel about yourself to others. So this question about how you see yourself is very important. If you see yourself as a champion who wins every fight, that is exactly how others will see you. But if you see yourself as someone who struggles and wrestles with a bad self-image — that is precisely how others will perceive you.

So let's turn to Romans 8:37 to see what the Word of God has to say about us. In this verse, Paul declares that "...we are more than conquerors through him that loved us." I want to especially draw your attention to the phrase "more than conquerors." It comes from the Greek word hupernikos, a compound of the words *huper* and *nikos.* By joining the words *huper* and *nikos* together into one word, Paul is making one fabulous, jammed-packed, power-filled statement about you and me!

The words "more than" are derived from the Greek word *huper,* which literally means *over, above,* and *beyond.* It depicts something that is way beyond measure. It carries the idea of *superiority — something that is utmost, paramount, foremost, first-rate, first-class, and top-notch; greater, higher, and better than; superior to; preeminent, dominant, and incomparable; more than a match for; unsurpassed, unequaled, and unrivaled by any person or thing.*

Now Paul uses this same word to denote what kind of conquerors we are in Jesus Christ. We are *huper-conquerors!* Paul uses this word *huper* to dramatize our victory.

This is what Paul meant to get across in Romans 8:37:

"We are greater conquerors, superior conquerors, higher and better conquerors!"

"We are more than a match for any foe!" "We are utmost conquerors, paramount conquerors, top-notch conquerors, unsurpassed conquerors, unequaled and unrivaled conquerors!"

But we must continue to the next part of the verse, where Paul calls us "conquerors." The word "conqueror" is from the Greek word *nikos*. The word *nikos* describes *an overcomer; a conqueror, champion, victor,* or *master*. It is the picture of *an overwhelming, prevailing force*. However, the word *nikos* alone wasn't strong enough to make Paul's point, so he joined the words *huper* and *nikos* together to make his point even stronger!

When you put these two words together, they form the word *hupernikos*, which declares that in Jesus Christ, you are *an overwhelming conqueror, a paramount victor,* or *an enormous overcomer*. This word is so power-packed that one could interpret it as *a phenomenal, walloping, conquering force!*

That's precisely who you are in Jesus Christ! So stop looking at yourself as a struggling loser. Regardless of your past experiences, you must begin to look at yourself through God's eyes and in the light of Romans 8:37. This verse declares that you are always the winner and never a loser! And when you begin to see yourself the way God sees you, it will change the way others see you too.

Resolve right now to see yourself the way the Word of God does — as a walloping and conquering force! You are more than a match for any adversary or foe that would come against you today!

My Prayer for Today

Lord, I thank You for making me a phenomenal, walloping, conquering force! Because of what Jesus has done for me, I am no longer a struggling loser. Instead, I possess the power to be an enormous overcomer! Holy Spirit, I ask You to help me take my eyes off my past failures so I can focus on the power of the resurrection that lives inside me. I pray this in Jesus' name!

My Confession for Today

I boldly declare that in Jesus Christ, I am a conqueror who is utmost, paramount, foremost, first-rate, first-class, and top-notch; greater, higher, and better than; superior to; preeminent, dominant, incomparable; more than a match for; unsurpassed, unequaled, and unrivaled by any challenge that would ever try to come against me! I declare this by faith in Jesus' name!

Questions for You to Consider

1. How do you honestly see yourself in life — as a winner or a loser?

   _____

   _____

   _____

   _____

   _____

   _____

2. Think about the Christians you know who exude boldness and confidence in the Lord. What do those people do to maintain that sense of confidence on a consistent basis?

   _____

   _____

   _____

   _____

   _____

   _____

3. What steps can you take to begin to see yourself as God sees you according to His Word?

_____

_____

_____

_____

_____

_____

Day 15

What Triggers a Demonic Attack?

> *Whereunto I am appointed a preacher, and an apostle, and a teacher of the Gentiles. For the which cause I also suffer these things....*
>
> — 2 Timothy 1:11,12

What triggers demonic attacks against you, your dream, your vision, your calling, your business, your family, your church, or your ministry? What makes the devil so upset that he rises up to resist you and your efforts? If God chose you, why are you experiencing so many hassles and difficulties along the way to your goal of fulfilling all He has called you to do?

In Second Timothy 1:11 and 12, Paul gives us incredible insight into what triggers a demonic attack. He says, "Whereunto I am appointed a preacher, and an apostle, and a teacher of the Gentiles. For the which cause I also suffer these things...." In this verse, Paul writes about his specific calling in the Body of Christ. He affirms to us that he is called and appointed to be a preacher, an apostle, and a teacher of the Gentiles. Then notice that he immediately follows by saying, "For the which cause I also suffer these things..." (2 Timothy 1:12).

The word "suffer" is the Greek word *pascho,* and first and foremost it means *to suffer as a result of outside forces or outside circumstances.* It could include *physical suffering* due to persecution; *mental suffering* due to outside pressures; *financial suffering* due to monetary hardships; or *any inconvenience* that stems from something outside of oneself or outside of one's control. Thus, the word *pascho* would depict any *suffering* or *inconvenience* due to forces beyond oneself.

When Paul wrote this verse, he used a tense in the Greek that lets us know he was experiencing these inconveniences at the very moment he was writing this epistle. At that time, Paul was in Rome, sitting in a prison cell, awaiting his own execution, and being accused of crimes that he had not committed. Because Satan couldn't find a way to personally destroy Paul, the enemy was manipulating outside forces against Paul and his ministry. The apostle's situation had been created by outside pressures that had nothing to do with himself but that the devil had orchestrated to use against him.

Satan was terrified of Paul's calling! The reason Paul was recurrently attacked is that the devil was fearful of the enormous progress Paul would make if he didn't face opposition. Paul let us know that his anointing, his calling, and his potential were the factors that triggered these demonic attacks. It's almost as though Paul was saying, *"Do you want to know why I've suffered so many crazy things during the course of my ministry? Because I am appointed a preacher, an apostle, and a teacher of the Gentiles."*

You see, Satan was scared stiff of what would happen if Paul operated 100 percent in his call. How much would he be able to accomplish if he had no resistance? If Paul was able to do the incredible things he did for God's Kingdom in the face of such opposition, what kind of Gospel advancements would he make if there was no opposition? This thought was so chilling to the devil that he threw every possible obstacle in Paul's path to slow him down, to discredit him, to destroy his friendships, and, if possible, to even kill him. *Satan hated the call on Paul's life.*

The reason Paul was never defeated by these attacks is that he had made a decision. He decided he would not stop or give up until he had apprehended that for which Christ Jesus had apprehended him (Philippians 3:12). Likewise, the only way you'll be able to resist the devil's attacks and successfully achieve all God has called you to do is by determining never to stop until you have accomplished your divine assignment. Jesus taught that those who "endure to the end" are the ones who will receive the prize (Matthew 24:13).

If you want to overcome all the attacks the devil tries to wage against you through outside forces, you will have to be determined to outlast every attack! *Determination is a key factor in finishing one's race of faith.*

Of course, no one can successfully resist the devil's attacks without the power of the Holy Spirit, but neither is the power of the Holy Spirit enough by itself. For that power to be effective, it must work in a committed person. God's power works in people who have resolve. It works proficiently through people who have decided they will never turn back until the assignment is finished. God delights in using people who are steadfast and unmoving in their conviction, tenacious and diehard in their commitment. He takes pleasure in those who have stamina, spunk, and a dogged determination to hold on to the vision He put in their hearts.

The most common reason people don't make it all the way to the end is that they weren't totally committed to completing the task assigned to them. Maybe they tried it or gave it a shot, but their commitment wasn't strong enough, and that's why they didn't make it.

There are many things Satan can do to try to elbow us out of the race, but the only one who can decide to *quit* is you or me. *Satan can't make us quit.* That choice lies in our hands alone.

If you make the decision to stay in faith and "slug it out" with the power of God at your side, you can do exactly what God called you to do. But you must begin with a rock-solid, hard-core decision to do it, do it, and keep doing it until it's done. *Make any lesser choice, and you will never fulfill your God-given purpose.*

My Prayer for Today

Lord, help me stay focused on my calling and remain determined to do what You've told me to do, even if I am assaulted by outside forces that seem to be beyond my control. I know the devil hopes to slow me down or even to stop me by orchestrating outside pressures to come against me. But I also know that Your Spirit works mightily in me, giving me all the power I need to resist every assault the devil tries to bring against me. Help me to be completely determined and committed to keep pushing ahead and to never let go until I've accomplished my God-given mission! I pray this in Jesus' name!

My Confession for Today

I boldly confess that I will not stop or give up until I have apprehended that for which Christ Jesus apprehended me! I will resist the devil's attacks and successfully achieve all God has called me to do, for I have determined that I will never stop until I have finished the task. I have the stamina, spunk, and doggedness it takes to get the job done. I have made the decision to stay in faith and slug it out with the power of God at my side. I can and will do exactly what God called me to do! I declare this by faith in Jesus' name!

Questions for You to Consider

1. What are the outside forces that Satan has tried to use to hinder you? Has it been your health, your job, your children, your family, your finances? What is the one thing Satan seems to use repeatedly as he tries to resist you?

_____

_____

_____

_____

_____

_____

2. When you are aware that the devil is trying to use events, circumstances, or people to slow you down or to distract you from your calling, how do you respond to these attacks? What steps do you take to overcome them and to stay on track?

_____

_____

_____

_____

_____

_____

3. Do you seek the strength and counsel of other believers when these attacks occur, or do you usually slug it out silently on your own? Judging by the outcome when you go through these difficult times alone, do you think you need to seek the strength and counsel of others more often?

_____

_____

_____

_____

_____

_____

Day 16

Are You Resisting the Devil?

> *...Resist the devil, and he will flee from you.*
>
> — James 4:7

When the devil tries to assault your mind, telling you that your God-given dream will never come to pass, how do you resist those assaults? Do you stand firm against those lies and command them to leave? Or do you allow the devil to mentally assail your mind with untrue allegations?

In James 4:7, the Bible tells us, "...Resist the devil, and he will flee from you." The word "resist" is from the Greek word *anthistemi,* which is a compound of the words *anti* and *istimi*. The word *anti* means *against,* as *to oppose something*. The word *istimi* means *to stand*. When placed into one word, thus forming the word *anthistemi,* it means *to stand against* or *to stand in opposition*. It is a word that *demonstrates the attitude of one who is fiercely opposed to something and therefore determines that he will do everything within his power to resist it, to stand against it, and to defy its operation.*

By using this word, James plainly lets us know that we must be aggressively determined to stand against the work of the devil. Just shutting our eyes and hoping the enemy will withdraw won't work. We must dig in our heels, brace ourselves for a fight, and put our full force forward to drive him back and out of our lives. Our stand against Satan must be firm, unyielding, and steadfast if we want to successfully resist his bombardment of lies against our minds and emotions.

Notice that James says we are to resist the "devil." As noted in many other *Sparkling Gems,* the word "devil" is the translation of the word *diabolos,* which is more of a job description than it is a name. You see, if you understand the word "devil," you also know exactly how this sinister enemy works.

The word "devil" is a compound of the words *dia* and *ballo.* The word *dia* has many meanings, depending on how it is used. However, in this particular case, it means *through,* as *to pierce something from one side all the way through to the other side.* The word *ballo* means *to throw,* as when a person throws a ball, a rock, or some other object. When these two words are joined, it means *to repetitiously throw something — striking again and again and again until the object being struck has finally been completely penetrated.*

Now do you see why this word is a vivid job description for the devil? It tells us exactly how he operates. He comes to assault the mind — not once but many times. He strikes the mind and emotions again and again and again. He just keeps on striking until he wears down the resistance of the one being assaulted. Then as soon as the victim lets down his mental resistance, the devil gives one last firm punch that finally succeeds in penetrating his mind. Once the devil has gained access into that person's mind, he begins to deluge him with lies on top of lies. If the person listens to those lies and believes them, the devil can then successfully build a stronghold in his life from which he can begin to control and manipulate him.

Does this kind of mental attack sound familiar? Well, let me ask you a question: Instead of giving the devil the pleasure of filling your head with a barrage of lies, why don't you start to resist him? That's right — just tell the devil to shut up and to stop dropping those dim-witted religious thoughts of nonsense into your head! Tell him to hit the road!

It's time for you to resist the enemy of your soul. Let him know that you're not going to bite that bait anymore, so he may as well go fishing somewhere else. You're no longer going to be a sucker! You have just been informed that there is a deadly hook inside that bait that is designed to hook you, pull you into the devil's net, and turn you into dead meat for the devil to chomp on for a long time. *But he has hooked you with that bait for the last time!*

James 4:7 has good news for you. It says that if you will resist the devil, he will "flee" from you. The word "flee" in Greek is so exciting! It is from the word *pheugo,* which from the earliest times of Greek literature meant *to flee* or *to take flight.* It was used to *depict a lawbreaker who flees in terror from a nation where he broke the law.* The reason he flees so quickly is that he wants to escape the prosecution process. Remaining in the nation would most assuredly mean judgment; so rather than stay and face the consequences, the lawbreaker flees for his life.

This means the devil knows that he is a lawbreaker! He also knows that if a believer stands against him — in other words, if the believer resists the enemy by using his God-given authority in the name of Jesus and with the Word of God — it won't be long until that believer begins to rule and dominate the devil. Rather than allow this to happen, the devil begins to withdraw and look for a way to escape the prosecution process. Instead of sticking around and trying hopelessly to defend himself against the name of Jesus and the Word of God, the devil tucks his tail and runs! That is precisely what James means when he says that the devil will "flee."

An expanded and more contemporary interpretation of James 4:7 could read:

"Stand firmly against the devil! That's right — be unbending and unyielding in the way you resist him so that he knows he is up against a serious contender. If you'll take this kind of stand against him, he will tuck his tail and run like a criminal who knows the day of prosecution is upon him. Once you start resisting him, he'll flee from you in terror!"

Friend, the devil wants to make your life less-than-gratifying, unhappy, and uneventful. That's why he attacks your mind and tries to convince you that God's dream for your life will never come to pass. He desperately wants to convince you to settle for less than God's best in life. That's exactly why you *shouldn't* settle for anything less than God's best!

God has given you the name of Jesus and the promises of His Word, so it's time for you to close your ears to the devil's lies and start quoting the Word and commanding the devil to leave in Jesus' name. If you'll take this approach, the devil will not only shut up and stop telling you his lies, but he'll run from you in terror! *Don't you think it would be a good idea for you to get started quoting the Word of God and using the name of Jesus today?*

My Prayer for Today

Lord, because You have given me the promises of Your Word and the right to use Your name, I refuse to let the devil bombard my mind any longer. Right now I stand up to resist him, oppose him, and put him on the run. Devil, you will no longer have free access to my mind and emotions, for I am standing up to resist you. You better put on your running shoes, because if you stick around me, I intend to prosecute you with the full authority of God's Word! I tell you to GO in Jesus' name! And, Heavenly Father, I thank You so much for giving me the great privilege of using Your Word and the authority of Jesus' name! I pray this in Jesus' name!

My Confession for Today

I confess that I am not a weakling! I have the power of God, the Word of God, and the name of Jesus Christ at my disposal. When I step into the full authority God has given me, the devil knows that he must flee. I will not submit to the devil's lies. If he tries to stick around and harass me, I will enforce God's authority upon him! That's why I know he will start to flee when I stand up to resist him in Jesus' name. So right now, I am taking charge over my mind and commanding the devil to take flight! I declare this by faith in Jesus' name!

Questions for You to Consider

1. How do you respond when the devil tries to assault your mind with lies over and over again? Do you let him have free access to your thought life — or do you stand firm against those lies and command them to leave in Jesus' name?

_____

_____

_____

_____

_____

2. Can you remember a time in your life when, after rising up and taking authority over Satan's mental bombardment in the name of Jesus, you could immediately tell that the mental assault had stopped and that Satan had indeed tucked his tail and run from you?

_____

_____

_____

_____

_____

3. What steps can you take to prepare now before Satan launches the next mental assault? Wouldn't it be a good idea to build a strong arsenal of truth from God's Word by meditating on scriptures you can use as a sword against the enemy when taking authority over his attack?

_____

_____

_____

_____

_____

_____

Day 17

Abhor That Which Is Evil

> *...Abhor that which is evil; cleave to that which is good.*
>
> — Romans 12:9

Today I want to talk to you about some of the detrimental things you have been tolerating in your personal life. First, let's look at the illustration of television as an example of what you must do to keep evil out of your life.

Our family rarely watches television or movies, but when we do, we are very careful about what we allow to be broadcast into our home. Denise and I know it is part of our God-given responsibility as parents to keep evil from gaining access, for God designed the home to be a godly sanctuary for the family. Because we don't want evil to affect our family, Denise and I carefully guard what is viewed on the television in our home. Some may say that our approach is narrow, but the apostle Paul clearly instructed all believers to "...abhor that which is evil..." (Romans 12:9).

The word "abhor" is the Greek word *apostugeo,* which is a compound of the words *apo* and *stugeo.* The word *apo* means *away,* and the word *stugeo* means *to hate.* It describes *an intense dislike, an aversion,* or *a repugnance to something.* When the words *apo* and *stugeo* are compounded together, the new word conveys the notion of *a person who hates something so extremely that he literally backs away from it in disgust.* Thus, the King James Version translates it as the word "abhor" to reflect the feelings of a person who is so repulsed by something that he shuns and avoids it at all costs.

This means God expects your tolerance level for sin and evil to be very low. In fact, you should have such a repugnance for evil that you actively and continually guard against it from ever invading your life or your family.

But when we speak of evil, exactly what do we mean? Since Paul is the one who told us to "...abhor that which is evil...," let's look at this word "evil" in the Greek text to see what he was talking about.

The word "evil" is the word *poneros,* and it conveys the notion of *anything that is full of destruction, disaster, harm, or danger.* It includes not only that which is dangerous to the physical body, but also that which is dangerous to the spirit or mind. So Paul is urgently telling us that we should have no tolerance at all for anything that would endanger our bodies or that would do any kind of damage to our minds or spirits.

As human beings, we are usually careful to take care of ourselves physically. However, Paul is telling us that we need to take care of our spirits and minds just as diligently as we watch over the natural care of our human bodies.

You see, if your spirit and mind are invaded by information or images that are evil, the entrance of those images into your mind and spirit can wreak havoc in your life for years to come. Your mind is like a movie screen — and what you allow into your mind lives in your imagination for a very long time.

So instead of watching, reading, or listening to a lot of evil garbage that will clog up your mind for years, why not take a safer and smarter route? In other words, don't allow that garbage to enter your mind in the first place!

What are you to do instead? Paul says you need to *"...cleave to that which is good."* The word "cleave" is the Greek word *kollao,* which is the old Greek word that means *to glue* or *to cement something together.* This word denotes *a permanent connection.* It is the picture of two things that have been glued or cemented together, so tightly joined and bonded that they are now permanently connected and cannot be separated.

Let me illustrate the strength of the word *kollao.* A form of this word is used in Ephesians 5:31, where Paul teaches that a man should leave his father and mother and "be joined" unto his wife. Just as it takes work for a man and wife to cleave to each other and to become one in mind and heart, it will take effort on your part to be joined unto that which is "good." That word "good" is the Greek word *agathos,* the Greek word that describes *anything that is good, beneficial, or profitable for you.*

So when you take each of these Greek word meanings into consideration, Romans 12:9 could be interpreted to mean:

"You need to abhor and be disgusted with anything that would bring evil and harm to your physical, mental, or spiritual life. Instead of giving place to those destructive things, why don't you put your whole self forward to become more joined with that which is good and profitable for you?"

As you've read this *Sparkling Gem* today, has God's Spirit been speaking to you about the things you've been tolerating in your life for which you should have no tolerance? If the answer is yes, it's time for you to get into the Presence of God and ask Him to forgive you for permitting wrong influences in your life or home. Then make a concrete, firm decision to remove those wrong influences, and deliberately turn your attention toward the things that will bring you closer to the Lord.

There are so many good things you could be watching, reading, and listening to. So make the quality decision to shun all that is evil as you cleave to that which is good!

My Prayer for Today

Lord, I ask You to help me be sensitive to the influences I allow in my home and life. I realize that You have given me the responsibility to watch over my life and that I need to be careful about the information and images I allow to pass into my spirit and mind. Please help me recognize the influences that are acceptable and those that are not. When I am quickened in my spirit that what I am watching, reading, or hearing is unprofitable, give me the strength of will to turn it off, lay it down, or walk away from it. I pray this in Jesus' name!

My Confession for Today

I confess that I carefully guard what goes into my spirit and my mind because God has given me the responsibility to do so. Therefore, I will not permit any evil garbage into the domain of my life. By keeping my mind free of evil influences, I will protect my life and stop the devil from many of the attacks he would like to launch against me. I refuse to open the door and invite the enemy in by watching or listening to the wrong things. Instead, I will turn my attention to those influences that are good and profitable for me. I am going to put my whole heart and soul into meditating on that which will enrich my life and take me to a higher level. I declare this by faith in Jesus' name!

Questions for You to Consider

1. What are you allowing in your thought life that you know is unhealthy for you? Has the Spirit of God been telling you to remove that evil influence before it affects your spiritual life and your mental health?

_____

_____

_____

_____

_____

2. Are your children taking into their minds and spirits certain television programs or certain types of music and literature that are unhealthy for them? If yes, what are you going to do about it? Will you continue to tolerate and allow these evil influences until they eventually produce destructive fruit in the lives of your children? Or will you take the initiative to remove every evil influence in order to protect them?

_____

_____

_____

_____

_____

3. What good things can you cleave to in order to bring a strong positive influence into the sanctuary of your home?

_____

_____

_____

_____

_____

_____

Day 18

The Devil Can't Curse What God Has Blessed!

> *How shall I curse, whom God hath not cursed? or how shall I defy, whom the Lord hath not defied?*
>
> — Numbers 23:8

I want to share with you about an interesting character in the Bible who actually tried to curse God's people. He attempted unsuccessfully to do it multiple times — which proves that *the devil cannot curse what God has blessed!* The example of Balaam shows that witchcraft, divination, and curses simply have no impact on people who are walking with the Lord.

Let's learn more about this man named Balaam. There are numerous sources that describe his origin, but the Bible is our most solid source, and it identifies Balaam in Numbers 22. Balak, king of the Moabites, heard that Israel was approaching his territory. Balak feared that his kingdom would be defeated by Israel's army. Verse 5 states that Balak "...sent messengers therefore unto *Balaam....*"

Balaam's lineage is difficult to determine because the Bible doesn't tell us where his family came from. The greatest bulk of what is known about Balaam comes from ancient Jewish commentaries. These ancient sources affirm that he was well known in his time and that he played an influential role as a diviner and soothsayer. One Alexandrian commentator described Balaam as a "master" diviner and foreteller of great renown.[1]

The city of Alexandria was a long-time center of Egyptian witchcraft, sorcery, wizardry, enchantments, incantations, magic, and spells — and the educated Jewish scholars from this city were very familiar with these practices. They had seen occult practices during their sojourning in Egypt, and they knew the difference between a *mere apprentice* and a *master* of sorcery. Thus, for an Alexandrian Jew to write that Balaam was renowned for his dark skills indicates Balaam possessed a profound level of expertise as a master sorcerer.

The most famous Jewish scholar was Josephus, whose writings are still considered the most accurate extra-biblical historical account of Jewish history ever written. He wrote, in effect, that Balaam was among the greatest of the prophets at that time.[2] That is a remarkable statement, since Balaam lived during the same time as the prophet Moses. But whereas Moses was an instrument for the *power of God* in the earth, Balaam was an instrument through which *the kingdom of darkness* found access in the earthly realm.

The use of the word "prophet" in the writings of Josephus should not be misunderstood. In this context, "prophet" does not refer to a spokesman of God, such as Moses or Elijah, for Balaam's practices were diametrically opposed to the way God manifested Himself through His prophets. In fact, Deuteronomy 18:10-12 and Leviticus 19:26 enumerates God's prohibitions regarding occult practices, such as those practiced by Balaam. Josephus simply used the word "prophet" in a general sense to denote *one who was able to foresee the future.* Pagans often used this word "prophet" to denote anyone who was a vocal instrument of the spirit realm. In this sense of the word, Josephus' description of Balaam was very much in line with what the Bible tells us about this controversial "prophet."

According to Scripture, Balaam was a diviner who operated with powers of divination (*see* Numbers 22:7; 23:23). Other common names for "diviners" include *foretellers, seers, soothsayers, consulters of familiar spirits, enchanters, necromancers, wizards, witches, voices through which the spirit realm speaks, mediums,* and *clairvoyants.*

The ancient world was full of diviners, but it seems none was more notable than Balaam during his time. Balak's own kingdom of Moab almost certainly had a plethora of diviners. But because none was capable of cursing Israel, he sent emissaries nearly 400 miles to plead with Balaam to come and curse the people of Israel on his behalf.

If diviners enjoyed a past record of success, they could demand high prices for their divination, and Balak knew that hiring a sorcerer as notable as Balaam would be very expensive. However, the Moabite king was prepared to pay whatever sum was required to coax Balaam to come and curse Israel. Therefore, he sent his emissaries to Balaam, offering to "promote" him with "great honor" (*see* Numbers 22:17). Verse 18 implies that Balak was willing to pay Balaam a great fortune — perhaps even "a house full of silver and gold" — to perform this service of cursing a nation of people.

We know Balaam was revered as a great diviner and soothsayer, known far and wide for his abilities to bless or curse, because in Numbers 22:6 (*NKJV*), Balak told Balaam, "...For I know that he whom you bless is blessed, and he whom you curse is cursed." Balak was certain that Balaam would be able to curse Israel — *but Balaam could not do it.*

Balaam tried three times to speak a curse upon Israel, yet he did not have the power to do it. Balaam finally was forced to tell Balak, "How shall I curse, whom God hath not cursed? Or how shall I defy, whom the Lord hath not defied?" (Numbers 23:8). Scripture tells us that every time Balaam opened his mouth to speak a curse, a blessing came out instead (*see* Numbers 23:10-12). Finally, after failing repeatedly to place a curse on Israel, Balaam conceded that divination was no match for the power of God. It was at this point that he told Balak, "For there is no sorcery against Jacob, neither is there any divination against Israel..." (Numbers 23:23).

It was simply impossible for a curse to be pronounced where God had pronounced a blessing! It was true then, and the same is true today.

Balaam serves as a reminder of God's divine protection. Balaam — one of history's most famous sorcerers — was unable to penetrate God's protective shield that held fast and secure around His people. Even today, there are some who allege that people involved in the occult have the power to curse believers. However, Scripture clearly teaches that *no one* has the power to curse what God has blessed. The story of Balaam serves as a perpetual reminder that what God has blessed is *blessed,* and that fact cannot be reversed.

If you are in Christ and walking in obedience to God's Word, you are safe, secure, and sealed in the protective blood of Jesus — and the power of that divine protection can never be breached by someone operating under, or in cooperation with, the powers of Satan. You need never be fearful of any curse assailed against you or your loved one, no matter how dark or "powerful" the vessel through which the curse tries to come. The occult has never been, *and will never be,* a match for the power of God that is inside a believer. This is precisely why the apostle John wrote, "...*Greater* is he that is in you, than he that is in the world" (1 John 4:4)!

I encourage you today to cast off fear of the devil or fear of *anything* that anyone has told you about the possibility of being cursed. If you are in Christ, you are *the blessed of the Lord* — and what God has blessed, no one can curse!

My Prayer for Today

Father, I rejoice that because I am in Christ, I am the blessed of the Lord and protected by the blood of Jesus Christ. The devil does not have the power to curse what God has blessed. Holy Spirit, I receive Your help to walk in obedience to the Word of God and to shun anything that would violate the supernatural shield of protection that surrounds my life. I pray this in Jesus' name!

My Confession for Today

I confess that I am safe and shielded by the blood of Jesus Christ. When God placed me in Christ, He surrounded me with divine protection that cannot be breached. No demon, no devil, no evil worker has the power to speak any kind of curse on my life. I am curse-free because Jesus Christ bore the curse for me in every form, that I might become the blessed of God forevermore. I do not live in fear of the devil, and I rejoice that greater is He who is in me than he that is in the world! I declare this by faith in Jesus' name!

Questions for You to Consider

1. Had you ever considered the impossibility of Balaam's attempt to curse God's people? How does it affect you to know that there is no divination strong enough to work against the people of God?

_____

_____

_____

_____

_____

2. What did you learn about Balaam that you never knew before?

_____

_____

_____

_____

_____

3. Before today, did you think that Balaam was just a backslidden prophet of God or did you understand that he was a sorcerer? How does the truth of his identity affect your understanding of what took place?

_____

_____

_____

_____

_____

_____

Notes

1. Philo, *De Vita Moysis,* I. 48,

2. Josephus, Flavius. *Antiquities of the Jews,* IV.VI.2.

Day 19

The Holy Spirit's Role in Removing Obstacles From Our Lives

> *Likewise the Spirit also helpeth our infirmities: for we know not what we should pray for as we ought; but the Spirit itself maketh intercession for us with groanings which cannot be uttered.*
>
> — Romans 8:26

Has there ever been a time when you just didn't know how to pray about some kind of challenge, or when you were in a predicament and you didn't know how to get out of it? Maybe you've come before the Lord and prayed, "Father, I'm not even sure if I know what the desires of my heart are. Please help me pray."

We all experience moments like these at one time or another. That's why I want to share with you about the Holy Spirit's responsibility toward us regarding prayer. We find a wealth of information about this in Romans 8:26.

Romans 8:26 begins, "Likewise the Spirit also helpeth our infirmities: for we know not what we should pray for as we ought...." That word "helpeth" is extremely important because it conveys the idea of real partnership and cooperation and paints the picture of two individuals working together to get the job done. The Greek word translated "helpeth" is actually a compound of three Greek words. The first word is *sun,* meaning *to do something in conjunction with someone else.* The second word is *anti,* which means *against.* The third word is *lambano,* which means *to take* or *to receive.* When these three words are joined, the new word, *sunantilambano, means to take hold of something with someone else, gripping it together as tightly as possible, and throwing your combined weight against it to move it out of the way.*

For instance, suppose you walk out of your front door one morning and discover that someone has placed a huge boulder in the middle of your driveway during the night. You walk over and push on that boulder to move it out of your way, but it's too heavy and you can't budge it. Then you try to move it from the other direction, but no matter how much you tug and pull, you can't get the job done by yourself. So what do you do? You call a friend and ask him for help. He comes over, grabs hold of that boulder with you, and together the two of you press against it with all your strength until you have moved the boulder out of the way.

This Greek word *sunantilambano,* translated "helpeth," powerfully conveys this same idea of partnership and cooperation to remove an obstacle. It tells us that the Holy Spirit literally becomes one with us in the task of removing every obstacle. In the midst of our weaknesses when we are inadequate to get the job done, the Holy Spirit says, "Let me grab hold of that hindrance with you, and you and I will push against it together until it is moved completely out of your way."

In this way, prayer becomes a twofold partnership between you and the Holy Spirit. When that really becomes a revelation to your heart — when you realize that your prayers are not something you're responsible for alone — it will forever change your prayer life.

Verse 26 goes on to say, "Likewise the Spirit also helpeth our *infirmities....*" It is the Greek word *asthenia,* which would better be translated "weaknesses." It is used to describe people who are *sickly* or *ailing in their bodies, minds, or emotions.* Frequently it is also used to describe people who are *spiritually weak.*

Thus, we see that the Holy Spirit comes to help us because we are *asthenia.* We are simply too weak — physically, mentally, spiritually — and by ourselves we don't have what it takes to get the job done. This is why we need our Partner to help us. We simply cannot pray like we need to by ourselves. So the Holy Spirit comes to assist us in prayer, throwing His weight against our weaknesses to remove them from our lives. The truth is, according to this verse, we cannot remove anything from our lives without the Holy Spirit's assistance. And that is why He comes to bear this responsibility for us, assisting us in removing anything in our lives that is ailing — whether it is frailty in the body, a sickly mental state, or a weakness in our spiritual walk.

I don't know about you, but I'm thankful that the Holy Spirit is willing to become a Partner with me to remove those weaknesses when I'm not able to remove them by myself!

Romans 8:26 continues, "Likewise the Spirit also helpeth our infirmities: for we *know not* what we should pray for as we ought...." In other words, we just don't have the "know-how" when it comes to prayer. We confront situations in which we simply don't know how to accurately view or pray about a difficult situation or decision we're facing.

This verse says we know not "what" we should pray. That word "what" is a Greek word *ti,* which depicts *a very little thing.* This tells us that we don't know the fine points, the hidden problems, the intricate details of what is involved in the matter we're praying about. Left to ourselves, we simply don't have the ability to see the whole picture in a comprehensive view. We don't have the know-how to deal with the smallest details and the entirety of possible challenges and problems that might arise regarding the situation.

Is there a specific way to pray about each instance that comes into your life that will remove every obstacle and foil the enemy's strategies against you in that situation? The next phrase in verse 26 sheds some light on that question: "... For we know not what we should pray for *as we ought....*" That word "ought" comes from the Greek word *dei,* which means *necessary.* Thus, this phrase refers to something that *must* be a certain way. So this part of verse 26 could be translated, "...We do not know how to pray *according to the need, as is necessary to pray, or as that need exactly demands.*"

Some needs demand a different kind of prayer. And this verse here says that without the Holy Spirit's cooperation in prayer, we don't know how to pray as each need demands. But thank God, His Spirit comes to remove our weaknesses and to *help* us in our inadequacy to know what to pray!

How does the Holy Spirit actually help us? We know from the word "helpeth" that He partners with us in prayer, grabbing hold of the obstacle and pushing against it in conjunction with us to remove that satanic blockade. Now let's look at the very end of verse 26 to learn more about how He helps bear the responsibility in prayer for us: "...But the Spirit itself [Himself] maketh intercession for us with groanings which cannot be uttered."

The word "intercession" is an interesting word. It's the Greek word *huperen-tugchano,* which means *to fall into with.* It is the picture of a person who comes upon someone who has fallen into some kind of quandary. Upon discovering the trapped person's dilemma, he swiftly swings into action to rescue and deliver the one who is in trouble. This word *huperentugchano* also carries the idea of *coming together in experience or meeting with.* Finally, it can mean *to supplicate,* which denotes *a rescue operation in which one snatches and pulls a person out of imminent danger.* So we could translate the phrase, "the Spirit itself maketh intercession for us" this way: *"The Spirit Himself falls into our situation with us"; "the Spirit Himself meets us in a common experience";* or *"the Spirit Himself sup-plicates for us, rescuing us from our weaknesses."*

Here we gain more insight into the way the Holy Spirit comes to your aid. As you're walking through life, things may seem to be going fine. But then the devil digs one of his holes in the path ahead of you that you don't even know is there. You take a step, and before you know it, you fall headlong into the hole. Now you're all scuffed up, covered with dirt and bruises, trapped at the bottom of a pit.

You can do one of two things at this point. You can feel sorry for yourself and stay at the bottom of that pit — or you can say, "Holy Spirit, this is where You come in. I don't know how I got here, and I don't know how to get out of here. I need Your help!"

So let's say you choose the second option. What does the Holy Spirit do after He meets you in your common experience at the bottom of the hole? He begins to supplicate for you — to move on your behalf to rescue you. When you say, "Holy Spirit, I need You to help me," He answers, "That's what I'm here for. I am here to bear the responsibility of helping you in prayer." And there at the bottom of that pit, the Holy Spirit takes hold together with you in prayer against the hindrances that are preventing your deliverance.

Have you ever prayed when you're in the pits? Your zeal is not exactly at a high level at that point. You might feel discouraged and confused about why you fell into that hole in the first place. You're bruised and dirty, and you may have spent most of your prayer time voicing your negative emotions about the whole situation to the Lord. But then the Holy Spirit meets you right where you are in the midst of your trouble and begins to help you in your weakness. He says, "I'm here with you. I'm going to grab hold of this problem together with you, and we're going to press against it until it moves out of your life."

All of a sudden, something rises up on the inside of you, and you sense a renewed strength to go after that problem in prayer. You throw back your shoulders, lift up your head, and pick up the spiritual weapons God has given you to win this battle and overcome the enemy's strategies in your life!

What just happened to you? The Holy Spirit grabbed hold of your weaknesses and helped you push them out of the way! This is His responsibility. And He'll keep pressing with you against that problem you're facing until it is moved out of your life and you're out of that pit for good!

Aren't you thankful for this wonderful work of the Holy Spirit in your life? Whatever challenges you're facing in these uncertain times, of this you *can* be certain: Right now He is making intercession on your behalf, and He's not going to stop until every obstacle to your victory has been moved out of the way!

If you've been feeling like you've fallen into a pit and you don't know how to climb out, just remember who's down there with you, ready to help. Then begin to pray, knowing that the Spirit of God will make you strong where you are weak and help remove every obstacle that hinders your forward progress in Him.

My Prayer for Today

Father, I thank You for the insight I've gained into how the Holy Spirit comes to my aid. When it seems that I have fallen headlong into a hole, I can call out to the Holy Spirit for help and He will meet me in my experience. Thank You, Holy Spirit, for moving on my behalf to rescue me. At the bottom of every pit, You take hold together with me in prayer against the hindrances that attempt to prevent my deliverance until they move out of my life. Father God, I thank You for assuring my victory through the power of Your Spirit at work in me. I pray this in Jesus' name!

My Confession for Today

I confess that each time I say, "Holy Spirit, I need You to help me," He answers, "That's what I'm here for. I am here to bear the responsibility of helping you in prayer." If ever I happen to fall into a hole, or if I feel discouraged and confused about why I fell into that trap in the first place, the Holy Spirit meets me right where I am in the midst of my trouble and begins to help me in my weakness. The Holy Spirit is always here with me, and He grabs hold of my problem together with me. We press against it together until it moves out of my life completely! I declare this by faith in Jesus' name!

Questions for You to Consider

1. Have you ever experienced a moment when the Holy Spirit fell into a situation with you and interceded for you — rescuing you from an obstacle when you could not rescue yourself?

   _____

   _____

   _____

   _____

   _____

   _____

2. How would you describe it when the Holy Spirit has joined you as a Partner to bring forth your deliverance from an all-encompassing problem?

   _____

   _____

   _____

   _____

   _____

   _____

3. Do you know the delivering, empowering partnership of the Holy Spirit? If you've never experienced it yet but simply tried to get out of problems by yourself, why not start today to let the Holy Spirit step in as your deliver.

_____

_____

_____

_____

_____

_____

Day 20

Demonic Intelligence — No Match for the Power of Jesus!

> *And the evil spirit answered....*
>
> — Acts 19:15

In Acts 19 we see how seven exorcists attempted to add the name of Jesus to their repertoire of magical incantations. As the story unfolds, we find that the seven sons of Sceva had a major confrontation — *an unsuccessful one* — with a demon-possessed man in Ephesus. As noted earlier, these exorcists saw Paul successfully using the name of Jesus to exercise authority over demons. Hoping to expel demons from a man in Ephesus, they added the name of Jesus to their list of magical names, even though they had no personal relationship with Jesus.

According to Acts 19:15, their attempt was futile. In fact, the verse says that the demon indwelling the man challenged them: "And the evil spirit *answered* and *said,* Jesus I know, and Paul I know; but who are ye?"

The actual structure of the Greek text says, "And *answering,* the evil spirit *said....*" The Greek tense tells us this was *not a single answer;* rather, the demon spirit that possessed the man verbally responded to each attempt the seven exorcists made to drive it out. Thus, the spirit was answering each time they tried to use a new magical name, spell, or incantation to drive it out. This, of course, tells us that evil spirits have *intelligence* and the ability *to speak* and even *to converse.*

This ability of evil spirits to speak is evident in the four gospels and in the book of Acts. A study of the Scriptures makes it clear that demon spirits are intelligent:

- They can possess specific information about things, places, or people.

- They can know the names of people.

- They have the ability to indwell a human being and engage that person's vocal apparatus to terrorize others, to blaspheme, to challenge, to make requests, and to scream, shriek, and cry out.

Vivid examples of evil spirits possessing intelligence and having the ability to speak can be found in Matthew 8:29 and Mark 5:7-12, where we read about the demoniac of Gadara. This tortured man was indwelt by a legion of demons that demonstrated both *intelligence* and the *ability to speak.* Mark 1:23-25 relates another example of this phenomenon. In this instance, evil spirits in a man spoke so *freely* that Jesus had to command them to stop talking and be silent.

Then in Mark 1:34, we are told that many sick people and those possessed with demons gathered to be healed and delivered by Jesus. The evil spirits referred to in this verse were so *fluid in speech* that Jesus actually had to forbid them to speak so they wouldn't reveal who He was before the time. These are just a few New Testament examples demonstrating that demons have both intelligence and the ability to use the vocal organs of the person in whom they dwell.

Going back to Acts 19:15, we read that this man had an "evil spirit." All demons are evil, but the word "evil" in this verse is the word *poneros. If* used in connection with animals, the word *poneros* depicts *ferocious, savage, and dangerous beasts.* Likewise, when this Greek word is used to describe *spirits* that indwell people, these spirits are *ferocious, savage, dangerous,* and *malicious* to those in whom they dwell and bring harm and danger to those who are in close proximity to them.

First, the evil spirits often create harmful and self-injuring behavior. The New Testament has many examples of such savageness. One example is found in Luke 9:37-39, where Luke tells us of a boy who periodically experienced demonic attacks that were injurious. Luke described it like this: "And, lo, a spirit taketh him, and he suddenly crieth out; and it teareth him that he foameth again, and bruising him hardly departeth from him" (v. 39). Matthew related the same account in Matthew 17:14 and 15, adding that the evil spirit would hurl the boy into fire and water. This was *ferocious, savage, dangerous,* and *malicious* treatment by the demon spirit against the one it possessed.

Another example is found in Mark 5:5, where we find the demoniac of Gadara, who was continually wandering in the mountains and among the tombs, crying out and "cutting himself with stones." He continually wandered around that isolated region, crying out in pain and agony while slicing his body with sharp stones — and it was all the result of the "evil spirits" that indwelt him. It is no wonder that these spirits are called *poneros* in the Greek, for they truly are evil.

But this description of the destructive impact of demonic control in a person's life should not cause us any fear. In my years of ministry, I have occasionally found myself in a confrontation with a demonized person. Just like the stories referred to in the Bible, I have heard demons speak, and I have seen them exercise physical power beyond human ability. But in each case, I have also seen them *wilt* and *shrink* when the name of Jesus is employed against them. We must remember that Jesus taught, "And these signs shall follow them that believe; *In my name shall they cast out devils...*" (Mark 16:17).

If you really know Jesus as your Lord and Savior — if you are in Christ — you can be sure that you have authority over demonic powers in the power of His name. Unlike the exorcists who used magic and incantations to manipulate the spirit realm and failed, you are empowered by the Holy Spirit, and you are given the name of Jesus to take authority over and to cast out demons. You are empowered by the Spirit of God and have real God-given authority in the spirit realm!

I am so thankful that the Bible clearly shows us that demonic powers shrink back at the name of Jesus. In fact, spirits are so fearful of that name that James 2:19 says demons "tremble" in the presence of faith and the name of Jesus. The word "tremble" is the Greek word *phrisso,* which means *to bristle,* as when the hairs stand up on a person's neck when he is suddenly "spooked" or startled by an unexpected noise, etc.

This means that even though demons may have intelligence to speak and power to be able to put forth superhuman strength, none of that helps them when they find themselves in the presence of a believer exercising his authority by faith in the name of Jesus. That prospect sends them into shock, panic, and dismay. Figuratively, it causes the hair to stand up on their necks. It terrifies them!

As a believer, you have the Holy Spirit living in you and you have the name of Jesus Christ to use at your disposal. That means you are in a position to make demons tremble! And it doesn't stop there. You also have the power to cast them out in Jesus' name, just as promised by Christ in Mark 16:17.

So the next time you find yourself in the presence of evil, don't *you* shrink back in fear. Release your faith and lift your voice to take authority over the devil's strategies in the name of Jesus — and as you do, you'll send those evil, malevolent powers scurrying away in terror! Then as you release the peace and the love of God in Jesus' name, His power will go into operation to calm those who had been adversely affected by that demonic oppression and turn that situation completely around according to God's purposes and to His glory!

My Prayer for Today

Father, I am inspired and thankful to learn I have authority that is given to me because of my relationship with Jesus Christ and His matchless name that He has entrusted to me. When I encounter situations where demonic power is present, I thank You for giving me the boldness to take authority and to expel those powers in Jesus' name! I pray this in Jesus' name!

My Confession for Today

I confess that greater is He that is in me than he that is in the world. The devil is minor compared to the awesome power of Christ that indwells me. When I speak the name of Jesus, empowered by the Holy Spirit, the spirit-realm listens and obeys. I am in Christ, and Christ is in me. When I speak in Jesus' name against demon powers, it is like Christ is speaking through me! I declare this by faith in Jesus' name!

Questions for You to Consider

1. Have you ever had an experience with demonic intelligence like Acts 19:15 depicts? When was that experience, and what happened?

_____

_____

_____

_____

_____

2. What did you learn from today's *Sparkling Gem* that you never knew about demons and our authority over them? This is a very important subject for Christians, so we need to know what the Bible teaches (*see* Ephesians 6:10-18)!

_____

_____

_____

_____

_____

3. Have you ever had an experience binding or casting out a demon spirit? When did that happen? What was the result?

_____

_____

_____

_____

_____

_____

Day 21

A Demonic Recognition

> *And the evil spirit answered and said, Jesus I know, and Paul I know; but who are ye?*
>
> — Acts 19:15

The evil spirits in the demon-possessed man in Acts 19 were very familiar with both Jesus and the apostle Paul. However, the demons did *not* recognize the seven sons of Sceva who were trying to exercise authority over them. We can know this from the original Greek in Acts 19:15, where the evil spirit responded to the seven exorcists: "...Jesus *I know,* and Paul *I know;* but who are ye?"

The words translated "know" in those two phrases — "Jesus *I know*" and "Paul *I know*" — are two distinctly different words in the Greek text. In the phrase, "Jesus *I know,*" the word "know" is the Greek word *ginosko.* The word *ginosko* has a wide range of meanings, depending on the context in which it is used. The foremost meaning of *ginosko* was *to recognize a person or a thing, to acknowledge,* or *to have a full comprehension about the person or thing being acknowledged.* There is no question that the use of the word *ginosko* here means the wicked spirit that inhabited this man *admitted, conceded,* and *affirmed* that the name "Jesus" was *well known* to it. Like all evil spirits, this demon *was familiar* with Jesus — it *fully comprehended* and *acknowledged* who Jesus was — and had possessed this knowledge for a long time. So when the evil spirit said, "Jesus I know," it was saying, in effect, *"...Jesus I know and fully comprehend with absolute certainty...."*

On the other hand, in the phrase, "and Paul *I know,"* the word "know" is translated from a completely different Greek word. It is the word *epistamai,* which describes *a knowledge obtained by outward observation.* In other words, Paul's reputation was growing as one who had authority over demons, and it had captured the attention of the spirit world in Ephesus. Local demons were "tuning in" to observe Paul's activities.

The word *epistamai* implicitly reveals that the dark spirit world in Ephesus had recently become familiar with Paul's ministry. The apostle's activities were a great threat to the demonic forces over that city, and they were taken aback by his spiritual power. Therefore, the evil spirits of the territory were *scrutinizing* this newcomer and *carefully watching* him move through each situation as one who possessed great authority. This word *epistamai* also implies that these demonic spirits were *spying* and *conducting surveillance* on this newcomer who had invaded their dark stronghold — so they could stay aware of what Paul was doing and look for ways to oppose him. The word *epistamai* therefore carries the idea: *"...and Paul I know because I have recently become familiar with him by carefully following and observing his activities...."*

But then the evil spirit asked the seven sons of Sceva an interesting question: "But who are ye?" This question should be understood in the context of the entire verse. The reader should understand the text to mean: *"Jesus I know and fully comprehend with absolute certainty, and Paul I know because I have recently become familiar with him by carefully following and observing his activities. But I have no idea who you are! In fact, we know nothing about you! We don't recognize you or your authority at all!"*

One would think that demonic forces would recognize exorcists who regularly delved into occult practices; however, the evil spirit in the man didn't recognize these exorcists at all. But oh, what a glorious thought that this spirit knew the name of *Jesus* and knew *Paul* because Paul was in Christ and was an authorized user of Jesus' name!

You fit that description too! If you are *in Christ,* you are an authorized user of the name of Jesus and the power of the Holy Spirit! James 2:19 says that demons "tremble" when they hear that name. The word "tremble" would be better translated that they are "spooked" or "terrified" when they hear the name of Jesus spoken with bold faith by an authorized user!

If you are a Christian indwelt by the power of the Holy Spirit, you have all power in Heaven and earth given unto you (*see* Matthew 28:18). You are authorized to speak on behalf of Jesus and to take authority over any evil presence that comes your way. And it *must* obey!

My Prayer for Today

Father, I am thrilled and grateful to learn of the authority that I have in the name of Jesus Christ. I am so thankful that I am a real, born-again child of God — and that You have authorized me to use Your power and Your name at any moment that it is required. I need never be afraid of the devil because demons recognize that the power of God inside me is greater than all of them put together. Thank You for encouraging me to be bold when I sense the devil is trying to manifest his presence or wage an attack! I pray this in Jesus' name!

My Confession for Today

I declare that the Son of God lives inside me — and I am in Him — and when I am required to speak to an evil presence and command it to go, that evil spirit recognizes Jesus' voice speaking through me. I am not afraid. I do not give way to fear. I do not listen to communication that would incite anxiety or fear. I receive from strong, Word-based teaching resources, like this one today, in order to build my faith and prepare me to take action when it is needed! I declare this by faith in Jesus' name!

Questions for You to Consider

1. Have you ever thought about how sad it is that people involved in the occult are playing with powers that will ultimately work against them? Do you know someone personally who is operating under this kind of self-deceived influence?

_____

_____

_____

_____

_____

2. Demons know the name of Jesus — and if you are in Jesus, they know your name too. So let me ask you — have you ever had an experience where a demon spirit recognized you and obeyed your authority? Or have you heard of someone else who had that type of experience? Where was it, and what happened?

_____

_____

_____

_____

_____

3. How would you recognize a demonic presence in your immediate surroundings?

_____

_____

_____

_____

_____

_____

Day 22

Illegitimate Authority and a Demonic Attack

> *And the man in whom the evil spirit was leaped on them, and overcame them, and prevailed against them, so that they fled out of that house naked and wounded.*
>
> — Acts 19:16

As we continue looking at Acts 19, we find the evil spirit in this man was inflamed by the seven exorcists' feeble and ineffective attempts to cast it out. The evil spirit unexpectedly seized the full use of the possessed man's body to physically attack and injure them. Acts 19:16 tells us, "And the man in whom the evil spirit was *leaped* on them, and *overcame* them, and *prevailed* against them...." Those exorcists had encroached on demonic territory that they didn't know how to handle! Let's look at those words *leaped, overcame,* and *prevailed,* because they tell a huge part of this story.

When the text says the man "leaped" on them, it is the Greek word *ephallomai,* which means *to leap upon, to jump upon, or to pounce upon,* as a panther leaps on a weak and defenseless animal. This word carries the idea of abruptly taking a victim by surprise, which means these exorcists were completely taken off guard by this attack. Not only did the demon-possessed man leap on them, but the verse also says that he "...overcame them, and prevailed against them...."

The word "overcame" is a translation of the word *katakurieuo,* a compound of the words *kata* and *kurios.* The word *kata* carries the idea of a force that is *dominating* or *subjugating,* and the word *kurios* is the Greek word for a *lord* or *master.* When compounded into one word, the new word means *to completely conquer, to master, to quash, to crush, to subdue, to defeat, to force into a humiliating submission,* or *to bring one to his knees in surrender.*

The word *katakurieuo* leaves no room for misunderstanding — this was a *humiliating defeat* for these seven exorcists. Their defeat was so complete that the verse goes on to say that the evil spirit *"prevailed* against them." The word "prevail" is a translation of the Greek word *ischuos,* which describes a *mighty* individual, such as a man with such muscular strength or physical power that he could defeat any opponent.

It is indisputably clear that evil spirits have the ability to supernaturally energize those in whom they dwell. When they do, the demonized individuals may exhibit inexplicable physical strength. One of the best examples of this is found in Mark 5:3,4. Here we read again about the demoniac of Gadara, who was so supernaturally energized that no one could bind him, not even with fetters and chains. If people were successful enough to attach the fetters and chains around this man, he was so empowered by demons that he could tear those heavy iron chains to pieces and get free almost without effort. Absolutely no one could tame him or bring him under control — *except* Jesus.

The demons that inhabited this man who lived among the tombs in the Gadarenes were violent beyond any human's ability to control. It must be noted that ancient Greek literature used the word *daimonian* — the word "demon" — to portray a person who is *mad* or *insane*. But this is not only the classical Greek view. The New Testament also shows that those who were possessed with evil spirits were mad and often afflicted with *physical illnesses*. This is why Matthew 4:24 says, "...They brought unto him [Jesus] all sick people that were taken with divers diseases and torments, and those which were possessed with devils, and those which were lunatick, and those that had the palsy; and he healed them."

Please get the revelation of this, because it is crucial. Jesus had *absolute* authority over evil spirits when He walked this earth. Then He gave the authority to cast out demons in His name to all those who trust in Him (*see* Mark 16:17). *This was the secret of Paul's success.* But these seven sons of Sceva were *not* believers; they were simply exorcists trying a new formula. And they soon discovered what happens to those who try to wield spiritual authority they don't possess. Those men were *no* match for the demons that indwelt the demoniac at Ephesus!

As the seven exorcists commanded the evil spirit to leave the man, suddenly the evil spirit seized the man's body and demonically energized it, and the man surged forward like a fierce wild animal and pounced upon them. After being severely beaten and battered, all seven of those men fled the scene in fear. Verse 16 says, "...They fled out of that house naked and wounded."

The word "fled" in Greek is *ekpheugo.* This word is a compound of the word *ek* — meaning *out,* as *to exit* or *leave a place* — and the word *pheugo,* which means *to flee* or *to run swiftly.* When these two words are compounded, the new word conveys the idea that those seven sons of Sceva *got out* of the house *as quickly as they possibly could,* making a mad dash or *a fast exit.* And no wonder they wanted to get out so quickly — they had been injured and had even lost their clothes in the attack!

The verse says the seven men fled out of "that house," referring to the house where the demoniac was kept. The wording of this phrase implies that this was a well-known house. It wasn't just a house; it was the house where this savage man lived. It was the place everyone avoided and stayed far from, for too much fear was associated with it and with the violent activities that took place there. And at that moment, it was the exorcists themselves who were escaping from "that house" in great haste!

When the men ran out of the house, Acts 19:16 says they were "naked and wounded." The word "naked" is *gumnos,* an often-used Greek word that simply means *physically naked.* The word "wounded" is *traumatidzo,* which means *to cause injury or harm* and is where we get the words trauma and traumatized.

We don't know the exact details of this demonic attack, how long it lasted, or how badly these seven sons of Sceva suffered. We do know, however, that by the time they exited the house, they were *naked, physically wounded,* and *traumatized.*

When people heard that these particular exorcists had miserably failed to exorcise the demon, it was big news in Ephesus. Everyone heard how the evil spirit acknowledged the name and authority of Jesus and even knew the name of Paul, Christ's servant — yet did *not* recognize these famous professional exorcists. So even in this worst-case demonic scenario, God's purposes prevailed as it was noised abroad that only the name of Jesus had been recognized and respected by the demon world, bringing attention to that name all over the city of Ephesus and throughout the surrounding region (*see* Acts 19:17).

I assure you that the kingdom of darkness knows your name as well. As a child of God, you have the legitimate authority to wield the name of Jesus like a weapon in your hand against everything the enemy might try to throw at you. And when you exercise that authority in faith, every demon that has been sent to harass you will flee in terror! *Hell knows you and trembles when you stand in the power of the name of Jesus!*

My Prayer for Today

Father, what an awesome thing to realize that the demons not only recognize Jesus' authority — they also recognize the authority of those who know Jesus. Of course, Jesus stripped Satan of all his powers (Colossians 2:15) and it should be no surprise to me that he is terrified of Jesus' name and those who had been authorized to use it. But I am especially thankful to You for bringing me out of the bondage of darkness, for translating me into the kingdom of Your dear Son, and for giving me authority in the name of Jesus Christ! I pray this in Jesus' name!

My Confession for Today

Demons may have authority over unsaved people, but I boldly confess they do not have authority over me and others who are in Christ Jesus. I never have to fear a demonic attack like the seven sons of Sceva experienced because the devil is the one who is running from me when I use the Spirit-empowered name of Jesus! I refuse to shrink in fear, and I refuse to let the devil intimidate me, because I have the presence of the Greater One living inside me! I declare this by faith in Jesus' name!

Questions for You to Consider

1. In your lifetime, have you ever heard of anyone who came under a demonic attack similar to the one we read about in Acts 19:16 today?

   _____

   _____

   _____

   _____

   _____

2. I once had a demon-inflicted man pick up a table and try to throw it at me, but he strictly obeyed me and put it down when I authoritatively spoke to him in the name of Jesus. Have you had any experiences where demons have quickly obeyed when you used Jesus' name?

   _____

   _____

   _____

   _____

   _____

3. What faith-building stories can you recall of believers exercising authority over demon spirits?

_____

_____

_____

_____

_____

_____

Day 23

Here's What To Do if the Devil Is Trying To Devour You!

> *Be sober, be vigilant; because your adversary the devil, as a roaring lion, walketh about, seeking whom he may devour.*
>
> — 1 Peter 5:8

Has the devil ever tried to use your past against you? Maybe he's told you, "You're in this mess because of your own actions! Don't even try to ask God to help you because you got into this mess by yourself, and now you're going to have to get out of it by yourself! God won't help you, because you're reaping exactly what you've sown!"

If you have ever heard these kinds of accusations from the devil, then First Peter 5:8 is just for you! It says, "Be sober, be vigilant; because your adversary the devil, as a roaring lion, walketh about, seeking whom he may devour."

The word "vigilant" comes from the Greek word *gregoreo,* which means *to be on your guard, to be watchful,* or *to be attentive.* This word primarily denotes *the watchful attitude of one who is on the lookout to make certain no enemy or aggressor can successfully gain entry into his life or place of residence.*

This tells us that we must be on high alert against an enemy who is seeking to gain access to our lives. The Greek tense for the word "vigilant" means *to be continually, perpetually vigilant.* That means this is not a one-time act of vigilance, but the attitude of a person who is unwavering in his commitment. This person has resolved that he will never let up in his pledge to be *watchful, wide awake, and on the lookout* to make sure some sinister force doesn't successfully sneak up to attack and overtake him.

The fact that Peter uses the word *gregoreo* lets us know that the devil can be pretty sneaky in the way he attacks. Therefore, we must be *constantly observant* to keep the devil out of our affairs.

Peter goes on to say, "Be sober, be vigilant; because your *adversary....*" That word "adversary" is from the Greek word *antidikos.* This word was used in New Testament times for *a lawyer who argued in a court of law.* This was the picture of a *prosecutor* who brought offenders to court, argued vehemently against them, and then sent them off to prison. Now Peter uses this word to depict the way the devil may try to overtake us!

Peter is telling us that when the devil strikes, he often acts like a lawyer who tries to bring us down by prosecuting us with the facts of our past sins and mistakes. The enemy drags up facts from the past and reminds us of our former failures; then he vigorously tries to convince us that we deserve to be in the mess we are in. If the devil is successful in his prosecution, he will persuade us to believe that we are unrighteous and unworthy and that we deserve as just punishment whatever difficulties he is throwing our way.

It is unfortunate that many believers assist the devil in his efforts to prosecute them by being irresponsible or negligent in key areas of their lives. For instance, many people have money problems because they have spent too much money or used their credit cards way beyond the limit of what they could afford. Others get sick in the wintertime because they go outside without proper clothing. Marriages get into trouble because the spouses never spend time together or do anything to nurture their relationships. Christians like to blame the devil for everything that happens, but the truth is, people usually help out the enemy a little along the way!

Praise God, when we sin and do wrong, His grace is there to forgive and to restore us! But the devil is also there. The enemy remembers every innocent mistake made along the way, and like a prosecutor or "adversary" (the Greek word *antidikos*), he comes to accuse you. Like a lawyer, he argues his points in your mind, saying:

- *You're in this mess because of your own dumb mistakes!*

- *You're reaping what you sowed, and there's no way for you to get out of this mess!*

- *You're paying for your past!*

- *Your kids are a mess because you failed as a parent!*

- *You're going to go bankrupt because you spent too much money on worthless things!*

- *You've destroyed all your friendships because you weren't a faithful friend!*

Sometimes the devil is accurate in what he tells you. It may be true that you created this mess! You really may have messed up your friendships by not being a faithful friend. You may have spent too much money, and the financial trouble you're in now may very well be your own fault! All the devil's accusations may be true. Believe me, he isn't going to make up some absurd fantasy that won't affect you. *The devil is going to try to use facts and arguments that make sense to you so you'll agree with him!*

But you must never forget what David told us: The Lord is the One who redeems our lives from destruction (Psalm 103:4). He is a restoring, delivering, redeeming God! He wants to snatch you out of the power of darkness and get you over into His realm of life and light where past sin won't continue to exert its influences upon you (Colossians 1:13)! You just need to genuinely repent of past mistakes, get your heart right with God, and then tell the devil to flee!

If you keep dwelling on the accusations that the enemy is speaking against you in your mind, you'll find yourself in trouble pretty quickly. Peter goes on to tell you why this is so: "…The devil, as a roaring lion, walketh about, seeking whom he may devour."

Have you ever heard lions when they are hungry? They roar so loudly that the sound is nearly deafening. Peter says that this is what it's like when the devil starts attacking your mind. Your mind is so filled with the roars of the enemy's accusations that you can't hear anything else but those lies. He tells you over and over, *"You're going to fail…fail…fail…fail…FAIL!!!"* Even when people try to tell you the truth, it's hard to hear what they're saying because those lies are roaring so loudly in your mind and ears!

If you keep giving ear to the devil's accusations, he will keep you all torn up inside and in a constant state of turmoil. In fact, Peter says he will "devour" you. The word "devour" is the Greek word *pino,* which means *to drink, to lick, or to slurp up, as a lion might lick the blood of his prey off the ground.* The devil wants to turn you into a mess of liquid emotions and then lick you up until there's nothing left of your life. That's what he wants to do with you — but you don't have to let him do it!

When you put all these words together, First Peter 5:8 could be interpreted:

"You must be constantly alert and on your guard! The devil, like an accusing lawyer, will try to charge you with all kinds of arguments and accusations. You need to know that he is like a lion on the prowl — constantly walking around, roaring with a deafening sound, earnestly seeking the kind of person he can completely consume and slurp up!"

You don't have to fall victim to the devil's attacks! Peter tells us, "Whom resist stedfast in the faith..." (1 Peter 5:9). If you'll resist the devil, you can run him clear out of your mind and your life. He doesn't know how to deal with those who stand up to him, so he runs in fear when a believer challenges him! And if you feel too weak to resist the devil by yourself, I would advise you to find people who know how to pray and let them help you!

Has the devil been harassing you about anything in particular? Are you tired of this constant harassment? If so, it's time for you to stand up, throw back your shoulders, and command him to leave in Jesus' name! Then determine to stay alert and watchful, constantly on your guard. You can be sure that the enemy will try to come back to accuse you again — but next time, you'll be ready for him!

My Prayer for Today

Lord, I am asking You to help me take authority over the accusations that the devil has been speaking in my mind. He's been telling me all the reasons that I shouldn't have any hope and that I deserve to be in this mess. But Your grace is greater than any mistake I've made or sin I've committed in the past! I know that You have forgiven me and redeemed me from any mess I've created by my own actions. I thank You now for Your forgiveness and mercy, and today I lay claim to the power of restoration! Devil, right now I command you to leave me in Jesus' name! I refuse to listen to your accusations any longer! I pray this in Jesus' name!

My Confession for Today

I declare that I have confessed all my past sins and mistakes. Therefore, I am forgiven; I am clean; and I am free in the sight of the Lord. He does not hold my past against me. He is my Redeemer, my Restorer, my Deliverer, and my Salvation. His Spirit is operating in me right now to get me out of every mess I have created, both intentionally and unintentionally. My heart is repentant, and my desire is to do what is right. Therefore, God is helping me walk out of the problems that have tried to grip my mind and my life! I declare this by faith in Jesus' name!

Questions for You to Consider

1. Are there areas in your life in which the devil is trying to drag up the past so he can accuse you and convince you that you deserve the attacks that are coming against you right now?

   _____

   _____

   _____

   _____

   _____

   _____

2. Have you taken the time to sincerely repent for those past sins and mistakes before the Lord? Or did you just quickly admit you sinned, never allowing the Holy Spirit to deal with you deeply about these matters?

   _____

   _____

   _____

   _____

   _____

   _____

3. If the devil has been roaring in your mind, consider what steps you can take to stop those roaring accusations, such as listening to praise and worship music or teaching, meditating on the Word, etc. What other steps can you take to silence the enemy's accusations?

    _____

    _____

    _____

    _____

    _____

    _____

Day 24

The Devil's Destination

> *Put on the whole armour of God, that ye may be able to stand against the wiles of the devil.*
>
> — Ephesians 6:11

What I am about to tell you is so simple — yet it is also life-changing and revolutionary. I want to help you understand how the devil tries to work in the realm of the mind and emotions. If you grab hold of these truths, they can set you free from the devil's lies forever!

In Ephesians 6:11, Paul explicitly tells us how the devil operates. He writes, "Put on the whole armour of God, that ye may be able to stand against the wiles of the devil." I want you to especially pay attention to the phrase "the wiles of the devil."

The word "wiles" is taken from the word *methodos.* It is a compound of the words *meta* and *odos.* The word *meta* is a preposition that means *with.* The word *odos* is the word for a *road.* When the words *meta* and *odos* are compounded into one word, as in Ephesians 6:11, it literally means *with a road.* You've probably already figured out that the word *methodos* is where we get the word "method." Some translations actually translate the word *methodos* as the word "method," but the word "method" is not strong enough to convey the full meaning of the Greek word *methodos.*

Let me make the meaning of this word real simple for you. As I said, the most literal meaning of the word "wiles" *(methodos)* is *with a road.* I realize this seems strange, but when you connect this to the devil as Paul does in Ephesians 6:11, it means that the devil is like *a traveler who travels on a road.* He is headed in one direction and has one destination.

Let me give you an example of what I mean. If you're going to take a trip, the logical thing for you to do is get your GPS and chart your journey to your destination. You don't take just any road; rather, you strategize to find the best and fastest way to get where you're going. *Right?* It would be pretty foolish for you to jump in the car and take off with no sense of direction. Taking any road could lead you in a multitude of wrong directions. It's just better to use your GPS and stay on track. *Correct?*

This is precisely the idea of the word *methodos.* The devil isn't wasting any time. He knows where he wants to go. He has chosen his destination. Rather than mess around on a bunch of different routes, he has mastered the best way to get where he wants to go. He is *not* a mindless traveler. And when he arrives at his place of destination, he has one main goal he wants to accomplish: He wants to wreak havoc and bring destruction. Therefore, we must ask: *"Where is the devil traveling, and what does he want to do once he gets there?"*

Paul answers the question about Satan's destination in Second Corinthians 2:11 when he says, "...we are not ignorant of his [Satan's] devices." Pay careful attention to the word "devices" in this verse. It is the Greek word *noemata,* a form of the word *nous.* The Greek word *nous* describes the *mind* or the *intellect.* Thus, in one sense Paul is saying, *"...we are not ignorant of the way Satan schemes and thinks."*

But the word *noemata* also denotes Satan's insidious plot to fill the human mind with *confusion.* There is no doubt that the mind is the arena where Satan feels most comfortable. He knows if he can access a person's mind and emotions, he will very likely be able to ensnare that individual in a trap. One writer says that the word *noemata* not only depicts Satan's scheming mind but also his crafty, subtle way of attacking and victimizing *others'* minds.

I personally like this because it identifies the primary destination of the devil — *to get into a person's mind and fill it with lying emotions, false perceptions, and confusion.* It was for this reason that Paul urged, "Casting down imaginations, and every high thing that exalteth itself against the knowledge of God, and bringing into captivity every thought to the obedience of Christ" (2 Corinthians 10:5).

The words "bringing into captivity" are from the Greek word *aichmalotidzo,* which pictured *a soldier who has captured an enemy and now leads him into captivity with the point of a sharpened spear thrust into the flesh in his back.* The captured enemy knows that if he tries to move or get away, the Roman soldier will shove that spear clear through his torso and kill him. Therefore, this captive doesn't dare move but remains silent, submissive, and non-resistant.

However, when Paul uses the word *aichmalotidzo* in this verse, he writes in a tense that describes the continuous action of taking such an enemy captive. This is not a one-time affair; it is the lifelong occupation of this soldier. He constantly has a spear in his hand, and he is always pushing it against the flesh of an enemy's backside as he leads him away to permanent captivity.

Because the devil loves to make a playground out of your mind and emotions, you must deal with him like a real enemy. Rather than fall victim to the devil's attacks, you must make a mental decision to seize every thought he tries to use to penetrate your mind and emotions. Rather than let those thoughts take you captive, you have to reach up and grab them and force them into submission! You must take *every* thought captive to the obedience of Christ!

But if you're going to beat the devil at his game, you have to put all your energy into taking every thought captive. If you're not really committed to seizing *every* thought the devil tries to inject into your mind and emotions, he'll strike you again! So once you make the decision to do it, stick with it. *It's time for you to take charge of your thoughts and drive his lying insinuations right out of your brain!*

My Prayer for Today

Lord, I don't want the devil to fill my mind with insinuations and lies. My mind belongs to You, and the devil has no right to flood me with false perceptions, vain imaginations, or lies about who I am or what I will never be. I refuse to let him operate in me any longer! You have provided me with the helmet of salvation, and by faith I put it on to protect my mind against the devil's assaults. He can strike as hard as he wishes, but Your Spirit and Word protect me! I pray this in Jesus' name!

My Confession for Today

I confess that I bring every thought into the captivity of Christ! When the devil tries to invade my mind with lies, I capture those lies and drive them clear out of my brain! Rather than fall victim to the devil's attacks, I seize every thought that he tries to use to penetrate my mind and emotions. I grab each lie and force it into submission! Because I stand firm on the Word, the enemy's lies are not able to exert any power against me. I declare this by faith in Jesus' name!

Questions for You to Consider

1. Can you think of one area in your mind where Satan repeatedly tries to attack you? What is that area, and how long has he been attacking you in this area of your thought life? Has it gone on for a day, a week, a month, a year, or for many years?

    _____

    _____

    _____

    _____

    _____

    _____

2. When you feel heavily assaulted in your mind and emotions and you need someone to pray with you, is there someone you know you can go to for prayer and support? If so, who is that person? If not, don't you think it would encourage you to find a friend to whom you could talk and who could help you resist the lies of the devil?

    _____

    _____

    _____

    _____

    _____

3. What is the most successful tactic you've learned to shut the devil up when he's trying to roar loudly inside your head?

_____

_____

_____

_____

_____

_____

Day 25

Don't Give Place to the Devil!

> *Neither give place to the devil.*
>
> — Ephesians 4:27

You and I never have to fall prey to the devil! If we can shut every door, close every window, and seal every place in our lives through which the enemy would try to access us, we can prevent him from getting into the middle of our affairs.

One of the "entry points" the devil tries to use to enter our lives is relationships. If there is an unresolved issue or an ugly conflict with a loved one or friend, these *conflict points* often become *entry points* through which the devil tries to get a foothold in our relationships with those we love. Once the enemy is able to slip in through one of these "cracks" and build an offended place in our minds, then a wall has already begun to be constructed that will eventually separate us from the people we need and love the most.

In Ephesians 4:27, the apostle Paul writes, "Neither give place to the devil." The word "place" is the Greek word *topos*. It refers to *a specific, marked-off, geographical location*. It carries the idea of a territory, province, region, zone, or geographical position. It is from this word that we get the word for a *topographical* map. Because the word *topos* depicts a geographical location, this lets us know that the devil is after every region and zone of our lives — *money, health, marriage, relationships, employment, business, and ministry*. He is so territorial that he wants it all. But to start his campaign to conquer all those areas of our lives, he must first find an *entry point* from which he can begin his campaign of unleashing his devilish destruction in our lives.

We often throw open the door to the devil when we:

- Refuse to let go of old hurts and wounds.

- Refuse to acknowledge what we did wrong.

- Refuse to forgive others for what they did.

- Refuse to stop judging others for their grievances.

- Refuse to admit we were wrong too.

- Refuse to say, "I'm sorry" when we're wrong.

- Refuse to lay down our "rights" for others.

If you and I do any of these things, we leave a "marked-off place" through which the devil can enter to accuse others in our minds. But we don't have to fall victim to the enemy's tactics. We can say, "No, you're not going to do this!"

We are more than conquerors through Jesus Christ, so we don't have to let the devil run all over us. The Bible boldly declares, "...Greater is he that is in you, than he that is in the world" (1 John 4:4).

The apostle Paul told us, "Neither give place to the devil." The Greek makes it clear that we must choose to give the devil no territory. You see, we have a choice: We can *choose* to "give the enemy place" in our minds and emotions, or we can choose to walk in the Spirit. If we choose the lower road, we will end up doing and saying things we later regret. Those regretful things are usually what opens the door for the devil to wreak havoc in our relationships.

I'm thinking specifically of a day I got very upset with one of our employees. I received information about one department of our ministry that really upset me. What upset me even more was that I believed one of our employees had known about this problem but hadn't conveyed the full truth to me about it. I scheduled a meeting to talk to that person the next morning to discuss this situation. That night as I lay in bed, I began to think about the problem we were facing. The longer I thought about it, the more angry I became that I hadn't been fully informed about the details as I should have been. I could feel a flash of heat pass through me as I kept pondering what to do next.

As I lay there in that bed, I began to take up an offense with this leader in our ministry. Once the devil got that foothold in my mind and emotions, it was as if a door had suddenly swung wide open for the devil to come in and begin accusing and slandering that precious employee to me. I tossed and turned all night long. I knew I could lay this issue down and walk in peace, or I could let it build in my mind until I became a walking time bomb. I chose to hold on to it and let it fester throughout the night.

The next morning when our meeting began, *I exploded!* My thinking was so distorted by the devil's ravings in my mind all night that I couldn't hear anything being said. I was *livid* with this employee. This employee couldn't even say anything, as I never even gave her ten seconds to respond to my accusations.

Later when the whole ordeal was over, I discovered that every detail of the problem had already been fully communicated to me. But I had been so busy at the time that I didn't even remember the conversation. Others on the staff remembered it very well. It was *my fault* that I didn't know and not *hers.*

I was so embarrassed that I had lost my temper. I asked my staff members for forgiveness, and they were spiritual enough to forgive me and allow me to be a man with real human frailties. *Thank God, our long-term relationship and commitment to work as a team overrides moments of human weakness that all of us display at one time or another.*

But there are *many* people who don't know how to recover from conflicts such as this one. Rather than face the situation head-on and either apologize or openly forgive, they hold their failure or their offense in their hearts, never forgetting it and never getting beyond it.

On the particular day that I exploded in anger, it was I who "gave place to the devil." As I tossed and turned in that bed the night before, I knew I was making a choice. I pondered the problem so long that I let anger well up inside of me and make my decision for me.

What about you? Have you ever given place to the devil by allowing anger, resentment, bitterness, or unforgiveness to have a "place" in you?

But let's look at the word "devil" for a moment. The word "devil" comes from the Greek word *diabolos,* an old compound word that is made from the words *dia* and *ballo.* This name is used sixty-one times in the New Testament. The first part of the word is the prefix *dia,* which means *through* and often carries the idea of *penetration.* Because *dia* is used at the first of this word, it tells us that the devil wants to make some kind of *penetration.*

We've already seen that the devil is looking for an *entry point.* Once a point has been located through which he can secretly slip into people's lives, he begins penetrating the mind and emotions to drive a wedge between those individuals and the other people in their lives. *The enemy's objective is to separate them from each other with his railing, accusing, slanderous accusations.*

You'll know when the accuser has gone to work in your mind because your whole perspective about the person you are upset with suddenly changes. You become *nit-picky, negative, and fault-finding.* You used to have high regard for that person, but now you can't see anything good about him at all. It's as if you've put on a special set of eyeglasses that are specially designed to reveal all his wicked, ugly, horrid details. Even if you do see something good in him, all the bad you see outweighs the good.

This is clear evidence that the work of the "accuser" has found an entry point to penetrate your relationship with that other person. He is trying to disrupt what has been a pleasant and gratifying relationship in your life. Don't allow that conflict, disagreement, or disappointment to cause you to pick up a wrong attitude that will ruin your relationship. That's exactly what the devil wants you to do!

Rather than allow this to happen, stop and tell yourself, *Okay, this isn't as big of a deal as I'm making it out to be. The devil is trying to find a place in my mind to get me to start mentally accusing that person, and I'm not going to let him do it.*

Instead of meditating on all the bad points of that person, *look in the mirror yourself!* Consider how many times you've let down other people; how many mistakes you've made in your relationships; the times you should have been held accountable but instead were shown unbelievable mercy. Remembering these things has a way of making you look at an offensive situation a little more mercifully.

Ask the Holy Spirit to take the criticism out of your heart and to cause the love of God in you to flow toward that other person or group of people. Pray for an opportunity to strengthen that relationship so all the entry places to your life and to that relationship remain sealed. Stop the devil from worming his way into the middle of your relationships with people you need and love!

My Prayer for Today

Lord, I ask You to help me keep the doors to my heart and soul closed to the devil! I know he would like to slip into my relationships and ruin them, so I am asking You to help me stay free of offense, free of unforgiveness, and free of bitterness. I realize these wrong attitudes create "entry points" through which the devil tries to gain territory in my relationships. I don't want to give the devil a foothold in my affairs through a wrong attitude. So I'm asking You, Lord, to help me identify every wrong feeling or attitude in my life that the devil could use to ruin relationships with people I need and love. I pray this in Jesus' name!

My Confession for Today

I confess that I walk in forgiveness! Offense, bitterness, strife, and unforgiveness have no place in my life. The Spirit of God dwells in me, and He always convicts me of wrong attitudes that the devil could potentially use to bind me. I love Jesus, and I want to please Him; therefore, I refuse to allow these destructive attitudes to remain in me. I am full of mercy, longsuffering, and slow to anger. All of these qualities keep me safe and secure from the devil's attempts to invade me. I declare this by faith in Jesus' name!

Questions for You to Consider

1. Can you recall a time when the devil got you all upset over something that wasn't really such a big deal? Did he stir you up so much that you couldn't sleep; you couldn't think straight; and you said or did things that you later regretted?

   _____

   _____

   _____

   _____

   _____

2. What did you learn from that experience? Did you see how the devil operates to toss you into a tizzy, steal your peace, and harm your relationships? If yes, how have you learned to keep the door closed so He can't access you this way again?

   _____

   _____

   _____

   _____

   _____

3. If you were counseling someone else who was struggling with a similar problem, how would you counsel that person to keep his heart free of bitterness, anger, or strife?

_____

_____

_____

_____

_____

_____

Day 26

Be Sure To Go to Sword Practice!

> *And take...the sword of the Spirit, which is the word of God.*
>
> — Ephesians 6:17

Have you ever been confronted with a situation where you felt you needed a word from the Lord, but you didn't know which word you needed? Did you run to your Bible and start flipping through the pages, searching for that perfect word you needed — but it seemed like you just couldn't quite find the right word to fit your situation?

Well, today I want to talk to you about the sword of the Spirit. You will find that when the Holy Spirit drops a word into your heart for your exact situation, that *rhema* word will have incredible power to drive back the enemy from his attack!

Let me begin by telling you a little bit about how Roman soldiers went to sword practice, because it will help you understand the difference between a *rhema,* or *a quickened, specific word from the Spirit*, and the *logos,* which is *the written Word of God.*

Because the Roman army was so committed to warfare, its soldiers practiced the arts of warfare *continually.* One of the primary exercises was daily sword practice. The soldiers exercised themselves in this skill morning and afternoon. The ancients gave their recruits bucklers that were woven with willow branches and were *two times heavier* than the ones used in actual battle.

In addition to these heavy bucklers, the swords that Roman soldiers used in practice were made of heavy wood and were *twice the weight* of the real swords used in battle. Every soldier practiced combat with a wooden post about six feet high, which was firmly fixed in the ground. This six-foot post became his "enemy" during practice. Just as with a real enemy, he would advance upon his target, strike hard with his sword, and then retreat.

The soldier's job in practice was to learn how to take advantage of his enemy; how to hit him at his weakest point; and how to strike him so he could not respond. The aim of the man wielding the sword was nearly always pointed toward the head or face, toward the thighs or legs, or occasionally toward the sides of the target.

Flavius Vegetius Renatus, who lived around 380 AD and who documented the affairs of the Roman military, wrote: "They [the military recruits] were likewise taught not to cut, but to thrust their swords. For the Romans not only made jest of those who fought with the edge of that weapon, but always found them an easy conquest. A stroke with the edges, though made with ever so much force, seldom kills, as the vital parts of the body are defended by both the bones and armor. On the contrary, a stab, although it penetrates but two inches, is generally fatal."[1]

It was from this background that Paul said, "And take...the sword of the Spirit, which is the word of God" (Ephesians 6:17). Notice particularly that Paul says, "...the sword of the Spirit, which is the word of God." The word translated "word" is not the Greek word *logos,* which would refer to the written Word. Instead, Paul employs the use of the Greek word *rhema.* This is so powerful — and I want to tell you why!

Had Paul used the word *logos* in this verse, he would have implied a "sweeping stroke" against the enemy, and this would never do. You see, the *logos* — although broad, heavy, wonderful, and full of general direction for our lives — is not sufficient to deal the enemy a fatal blow. We need to stab the enemy! This will require a *rhema — a specific, quickened word from the Scriptures, placed into our hearts and hands by the Holy Spirit.* With a *rhema* from God placed in our hearts and hands, we have real *sword power* to use against the enemy!

A genuine *rhema* doesn't have to be six pages long to be effective against the work of the devil. As Vegetius recorded in his history of the Roman army, all that was needed to kill an enemy was a mere two-inch penetration. Likewise, one very small *rhema* from the Lord has the power to do the adversary in!

The best example of this sword power of the Spirit is found in Luke 4:3-13. In this passage, Satan is the aggressor who is found attacking Jesus on repeated occasions. But Jesus doesn't simply say, "Satan, get out of here." *Instead, Jesus stabs the devil repeatedly with direct blows!* Jesus had a specific, quickened rhema from the Holy Spirit!

After the devil tempted Jesus with food, Jesus drew the sword that the Holy Spirit put in His hand (a rhema) and said, "...It is written, That man shall not live by bread alone, but by every word of God" (v. 4). *To this stabbing sword of the Spirit, the enemy had no response.*

After offering Jesus all the kingdoms of the world in exchange for worship, Satan was wounded deeply by one *rhema* from the Master's mouth. Jesus told him, "...It is written, Thou shalt worship the Lord thy God, and him only shalt thou serve" (v. 8). *To this sword of the Spirit, Satan had no answer.*

Then Satan tried to tempt Jesus to prove His deity. But Jesus answered His adversary with *a sword,* saying, "...It is said, Thou shalt not tempt the Lord thy God" (v. 12). *With one final stab, Jesus penetrated Satan's armor and delivered an almost fatal wound* — and at that point, Satan fled from the scene!

Like the Lord Jesus, you are equipped with all the armor of God, and this includes the sword of the Spirit. As long as you have this spiritual equipment, no battle is a real threat to you! Today if you will open your heart and listen, the Holy Spirit will place in your heart and hands the exact rhema you need to put the devil on the run!

My Prayer for Today

Lord, thank You for giving me the sword of the Spirit as part of my spiritual weaponry. When the devil attempts to attack me, please help me be sensitive to hear the exact rhema that the Holy Spirit desires to drop into my heart with which I can then deal the enemy a fatal blow. Starting right now, I open my heart and soul to listen so I can hear any scripture or word the Holy Spirit wishes to give me to use against the works of the devil in my life. I pray this in Jesus' name!

My Confession for Today

I confess that I have the sword of the Spirit, which is the Word of God, and that this spiritual weapon is working in my life! I have the exact word I need for every situation — a specific, quickened word from the Scriptures, placed in my heart by the Holy Spirit. Because this rhema from God is in my heart, I have real sword power to use against the enemy! I declare this by faith in Jesus' name!

Questions for You to Consider

1. Can you think of a time when you were facing a difficult situation — and suddenly it was as if God dropped a verse into your heart that had the very answer you needed? Did it equip you to deal with the challenge you were facing and cause the situation to turn around?

_____

_____

_____

_____

_____

_____

2. Why don't you think of three times in your life when you emphatically knew that God gave you a rhema for the particular situation you were facing? What were those times, and how did that rhema make a difference?

_____

_____

_____

_____

_____

_____

3. Are there any areas in your life right now where you could use a rhema from the Holy Spirit to help you know how to overcome a problem or a challenge?

_____

_____

_____

_____

_____

Note

[1] Flavius Vegetius Renatus, *The Military Institutions of the Romans*, trans. Lt. John Clark (Westport, Connecticut: Greenwood Press, 1944), pp. 20-21.

Day 27

The Holy Spirit Wants To Place a Razor-Sharp Sword in Your Hands

> *And take the helmet of salvation, and the sword of the Spirit, which is the word of God.*
>
> — Ephesians 6:17

How would you like God to give you a weapon that can rip to shreds the devil's strategies against you? Well, that's exactly what He has done! Ephesians 6:17 declares that God has given you "... the sword of the Spirit, which is the word of God"!

I want you to look at the word "sword" in this verse. It is the Greek word *machaira* — a word that exacted fear in the minds of those who heard it! You see, this wasn't just a sword, but a weapon of murder that caused the victim horrid pain as he lay bleeding to death.

Just for your knowledge, there were various types of swords used by the Roman army during New Testament times. For instance, there was a huge *double-handed sword* — a sword so massive that it could only be utilized with the use of *two hands.* This sword could not be used in real combat because it was too huge. Instead, it was used during sword practice sessions because it helped develop stronger muscles as soldiers swung it against a post that represented an enemy.

There was also a long sword that was used for fighting in a battle, similar to the sword we are familiar with today. This sword was very effective in battle, but it more often wounded the enemy than it killed him. Because it was long, it was most often swung at an enemy from the side, thus scraping or cutting a gouge into the side or limbs of an adversary.

But the weapon referred to in Ephesians 6:17, coming from the Greek word *machaira,* was neither of these swords. This sword was an exceptionally brutal weapon. Although it could be up to 19 inches in length, most often it was shorter and shaped like a dagger-type sword.

Just as a dagger is inserted into a victim at close range, this sword was used only in close combat. It was razor sharp on both sides of the blade. The tip of the sword often turned upward; sometimes it was even twisted, similar to a cork screw. Because this dagger-type sword was razor sharp, it could easily be thrust into the abdomen of an adversary. And if it had a cork-screw tip, the attacker could shred the insides of a victim by twisting the sword.

All these characteristics made the *machaira* a very deadly and frightful weapon. This two-edged, dagger-type sword inflicted a wound far worse than any other sword that was available to the Roman soldier at that time. Although the other swords were deadly, this one was a terror to the imagination!

By using the word *machaira* in Ephesians 6:17, the apostle Paul is saying that God has given the Church of Jesus Christ a weapon that is frightful to the devil and his forces. Why is this weapon so horrific to the kingdom of darkness? Because it has the razor-sharp power to slash our demonic foes to shreds!

Because the word *machaira* denoted a sword that was dagger-shaped, it tells us that the "sword of the Spirit" is a weapon that is normally employed in closer combat. Let's take this one step further, so we can understand why this is so.

Notice that this verse calls it "the sword of the Spirit, which is the word of God." The term "word" is taken from the Greek word *rhema,* which describes *something that is spoken clearly and vividly, in unmistakable terms and in undeniable language.* In the New Testament, the word *rhema* carries the idea of a *quickened word.*

Here's an example of a *rhema* or a *quickened word:* You are praying about a situation when suddenly a Bible verse rises from within your heart. In that moment, you know that God has supernaturally made you aware of a verse you can stand on and claim for your situation. When this happens, it's as if the Holy Spirit has put a sword in your hand — a spiritual dagger — that you can insert into the heart of the enemy to bring about his defeat.

There are many examples of God giving someone this kind of *quickened word* in the Bible, but the best one is found in Luke 4, where Jesus is being tempted by the devil in the wilderness. Over and over again, the devil tempted and tested Jesus. But with each temptation, a scripture was *quickened* inside Jesus, and He would speak forth that scripture to the devil, brandishing it like a sword against His enemy. Each time Jesus used a verse that the Spirit had *quickened* to Him, the sword of the Word dealt a serious blow to the enemy — causing the devil to eventually flee in defeat.

Because of the words *machaira* and *rhema*, Ephesians 6:17 conveys this impression:

"The Spirit will place a razor-sharp sword at your disposal anytime the enemy gets too close. This sword's power will be available the very moment the Spirit quickens a specific word for a specific situation you are facing."

When you receive a *rhema* from the Lord, the Holy Spirit drops a word or scripture into your heart, causing it to come alive supernaturally and impart special power and authority to you. This quickened word is so powerful that it is like a sword has been placed in your hands! That's why Paul calls it "the sword of the Spirit, which is the word of God."

The next time you find yourself in close combat with the enemy, take the time to get quiet in your heart and listen. The Holy Spirit will reach up from within your spirit and *quicken* to you a scripture that has the exact power you need for the situation you find yourself in at that moment. In other words, the Holy Spirit will give you a *rhema* — a specific word for a specific time and a specific purpose.

When that happens, you have just received real "sword power" in the realm of the Spirit. It's time for you to *insert, twist,* and *do damage* to the devil. Then you can watch in jubilation as he hits the road and flees!

My Prayer for Today

Lord, I know that Your Spirit has the very answer I need for any situation I may confront in life. When He speaks to my heart, it places a razor-sharp sword in my hands that I can use against my spiritual enemies. Help me keep a sensitive ear to the Holy Spirit so I can recognize those moments when He is trying to give me a "rhema" that will put the devil on the run! I pray this in Jesus' name!

My Confession for Today

I confess that I can hear the Holy Spirit's voice when He drops a word into my heart at the exact moment I need it. Those quickened words impart special power and authority to me. They are so powerful that it is as if a sword has been placed in my hands! When I receive that kind of word from the Lord, I insert it, twist it, and do as much damage as possible to the devil until he's sorry he ever messed with me! I declare this by faith in Jesus' name!

Questions for You to Consider

1. Can you think of times in your life when you needed a *rhema* for the situation you were facing?

   _____

   _____

   _____

   _____

   _____

   _____

2. Did you turn to the Holy Spirit in those situations to listen for a quickened word?

   _____

   _____

   _____

   _____

   _____

   _____

3. What steps can you take to help make the Scriptures more readily available in your life? How would that change the situation you are in now?

_____

_____

_____

_____

_____

_____

Day 28

You Have a Two-Edged Sword!

> *For the word of God is quick, and powerful, and sharper than any twoedged sword....*
>
> — Hebrews 4:12

What is the significance of the "two-edged sword" referred to in Hebrews 4:12? If you start looking, you'll find out this phrase regarding a "two-edged sword" appears all over the New Testament, so it must be pretty important.

For instance, when the apostle John received his vision of Jesus on the isle of Patmos, he said, "And he had in his right hand seven stars: and out of his mouth went a sharp twoedged sword: and his countenance was as the sun shineth in his strength" (Revelation 1:16). Notice that this "two-edged sword" came out of Jesus' mouth! Why would Jesus have a sword in His mouth? Shouldn't the sword have been in His *hand?*

The phrase "two-edged" is taken from the Greek word *distomos* and is unquestionably one of the oddest words in the entire New Testament. Why is it so odd? Because it is a compound of the word *di,* meaning *two,* and the word *stomos,* which is the Greek word for one's mouth. Thus, when these two words are compounded into one *(distomos),* they describe something that is *two-mouthed!* Don't you agree that this seems a little strange? So why would the Bible refer to the Word of God repeatedly as a "two-edged sword" or, literally, a *"two-mouthed sword"?*

The Word of God is like a sword that has two edges, cutting both ways and doing terrible damage to an aggressor. Ephesians 6:17 calls it "the sword of the Spirit, which is the word of God." As noted, the term "word" is taken from the Greek word *rhema,* which describes *something that is spoken clearly, vividly, in unmistakable terms and undeniable language.* In the New Testament, the word *rhema* carries the idea of a *quickened word.*

Here's an example of a *rhema* or a *quickened word:* You are praying about a situation, and suddenly a Bible verse rises up from inside your heart. At that moment, you are consciously aware that God has given you a verse to stand on and to claim for your situation. You've received a word that came right *out of the mouth of God* and dropped into your spirit! That word from God was so sharp that it cut right through your questions, intellect, and natural logic and lodged deep within your heart.

After you meditated on that *rhema,* or that quickened word from God, it suddenly began to release its power inside you. Soon you couldn't contain it any longer! Everything within you wanted *to declare* what God had said to you. You wanted *to say it.* You want to release it *out of your mouth!* And when you did, those powerful words were sent forth like a mighty blade to drive back the forces of hell that had been marshaled against you, your family, your business, your ministry, your finances, your relationship, or your body.

First, that word came out of the mouth of God. Next, it came out of *your* mouth! When it came out of your mouth, it became a sharp, "two-edged" — or literally, a "two-mouthed" — sword. One edge of this sword came into existence when the Word initially proceeded *out of God's mouth.* The second edge of this sword was added when the Word of God proceeded *out of YOUR mouth!*

The Word of God remains a one-bladed sword when it comes out of God's mouth and drops into your heart but is never released from your own mouth by faith. That supernatural word simply lies dormant in your heart, never becoming the two-edged sword God designed it to be.

But something happens in the realm of the Spirit when you finally rise up and begin to speak forth that word. The moment it comes out of your mouth, a second edge is added to the blade! Nothing is more powerful than a word that comes first from God's mouth and then from your mouth. You and God have come into agreement, and that agreement releases His mighty power into the situation at hand!

So begin to willfully take the Word into your spirit by meditating on it and giving it a place of top priority. This is how you take the first necessary step in giving the Word a "second edge" in your life. Then when you are confronted by a challenge from the demonic realm, the Holy Spirit will be able to reach down into the reservoir of God's Word you have stored up on the inside of you and pull up the exact scripture you need for that moment.

As that quickened *rhema* word from God begins to first fill your heart and mind and then comes out of your mouth, it becomes that "two-mouthed sword" described in the Scriptures. *That's* when demons start to tremble in terror!

My Prayer for Today

Lord, I know that Your Word has the power to defeat every adversary in my life. As I take it into my heart and get it deep into my soul, I know it will empower me to speak Your Word with mighty strength and authority. Forgive me for the times I have just skimmed over Your Word rather than planting it deep in my heart. I realize that the answers I seek are in Your Word — and that Your Word, when spoken from my mouth, releases authority against the devices the devil tries to use against me. So today, Lord, I make the decision to plant Your Word deep in my spirit man and then to speak it and release its power in my life! I pray this in Jesus' name!

My Confession for Today

I confess that God's Word is a mighty and sharp two-edged sword that releases His power when I speak it out of my mouth. I read the Word; I take it deeply into my heart; and then I release its power from my mouth to thwart the enemy's strategies and bring victory into every situation I'm facing today! I declare this by faith in Jesus' name!

Question for You to Consider

1. Can you remember a time when a specific scripture suddenly sprang up from down deep inside you, causing you to feel super-charged and empowered by God's Spirit?

_____

_____

_____

_____

_____

_____

2. When God speaks to you, do you first meditate on that rhema word and then let it come out of your mouth, or do you forget to speak that quickened word out loud and thus fail to release its power?

_____

_____

_____

_____

_____

_____

3. According to what you read today, what happens when you and God begin to speak the same thing?

_____

_____

_____

_____

_____

_____

Day 29

The Most Essential Weapon in Your Spiritual Arsenal

> *Stand therefore, having your loins girt about with truth....*
>
> — Ephesians 6:14

Roman soldiers were dressed in beautiful armor! From head to toe, they were covered with various pieces of weaponry that were designed to protect them and equip them for fighting. But of all these pieces, one piece was more important than all the others. That vital and most important piece of weaponry was the Roman soldier's loinbelt.

A loinbelt didn't look important. Certainly no soldier would have written home and told his parents, "Wow, I've got the most incredible loinbelt!" He might have told them about his shield, his sword, or his breastplate, but no one got excited about the loinbelt. Nevertheless, it was the Roman soldier's most important piece of weaponry. Why was this so? Because the loinbelt held many of the other pieces of weaponry together. If a soldier's loinbelt wasn't in place, he was in *big* trouble.

This is even true with modern clothing. For example, the belt I wear around my waist is not something people notice. They might mention my tie, my suit, my shirt, my sweater, and even my shoes. But to date, I've never had anyone walk up to me and say with excitement, "Wow, what a belt!" However, my belt *is* very important! If I removed it, I'd find out how important it is, because my pants would fall off! That makes my belt quite a vital part of my attire!

In the same way, the Roman soldier's loinbelt was the piece of armor that held all the other pieces together. His sword hung in a scabbard that was clipped to the side of his loinbelt. When not in use, his shield was hung on a special clip on the other side of his loinbelt. The pouch that carried his arrows rested on a small ledge attached to his loinbelt on his backside. Even his breastplate was attached in some places to his loinbelt.

Accordingly, the soldier's ability to use his other pieces of weaponry depended on his loinbelt. If he had no loinbelt, he had no place to attach his massive shield or to hang his sword. Without a loinbelt, there was nothing to rest his lance upon and nothing to keep his breastplate from flapping in the wind. The armor of a Roman soldier would literally come apart, piece by piece, if he didn't have the loinbelt around his waist.

You can see why the loinbelt was absolutely essential to the Roman soldier in order for him to be confident in battle. With that belt securely fastened, he could be assured that all the other pieces of his equipment would stay in place, enabling him to move quickly and fight with great fury.

Thus, the loinbelt was the most vital part of all the weaponry the Roman soldier wore. Now consider all this in light of Ephesians 6:14, where Paul says, "Stand therefore, *having your loins girt about with truth....*" For the child of God, the loinbelt of his spiritual armor is the written Word of God — the truth.

When God's Word has a central place in your life, you will have a sense of righteousness that covers you like a mighty breastplate. When God's Word is operating in your life, it gives you the sword you need — that *rhema* word quickened to your heart by the Holy Spirit. When God's Word dominates your thinking, it gives you peace that protects you from the attacks of the adversary and shields your mind like a powerful helmet.

As long as the loinbelt of truth — the Word of God — is central in your life, the rest of your spiritual armor will be effective. But the moment you begin to ignore God's Word and cease to apply it to your life on a daily basis, you'll start to lose your sense of righteousness and peace. You'll find that the devil will start attacking your mind more and more, trying to fill it with lies and vain imaginations. You see, when you remove God's Word from its rightful place at the very core of your life, it won't be long until you will begin to spiritually come apart at the seams!

If you want to stay clothed in your spiritual armor, you must begin by taking up God's Word and permanently affixing it to your life. You have to give the Word a central place and dominant role in your life, allowing it to be the "loinbelt" that holds the rest of your weaponry together.

So as you go about your daily routine today and every day, keep your "loinbelt of truth" fully attached and operative in every situation you face. Let the Bible be the governor, the law, the ruler, the "final say-so" in your life!

My Prayer for Today

Lord, I know that Your Word is the most important weapon You have given to me. Forgive me for the times I have not made it a priority in my life. Today I make the decision to never ignore Your Word again. Holy Spirit, help me stay true to this decision. Please remind me every day to open my Bible and take the time needed to wrap that Word around my life! I pray this in Jesus' name!

My Confession for Today

Because God's Word has a central place in my life, I have a sense of righteousness that covers me like a mighty breastplate. God's Word is operating in my life, giving me a powerful sword to wield against the enemy — that rhema word quickened by the Spirit of God to my heart in my time of need. And because God's Word also dominates my thinking, I have peace that protects me from the attacks of the adversary and shields my mind like a powerful helmet. I declare this by faith in Jesus' name!

Questions for You to Consider

1. Does the Word of God really have a central role in your life, or is reading your Bible something you do once in a while when it's convenient to you?

   _____

   _____

   _____

   _____

   _____

   _____

2. Was there a time in your life when you devoured the Word of God? What kind of fruit did that period of time produce in your life? Take the time to write down your answers and really think about them.

   _____

   _____

   _____

   _____

   _____

   _____

3. What changes do you need to make in your schedule now to give God's Word the central place it ought to have in your life?

_____

_____

_____

_____

_____

_____

Day 30

Are You Dressed in the Whole Armor of God?

> *Put on the whole armor of God, that ye may be able to stand against the wiles of the devil.*
>
> — Ephesians 6:11

Not far from our personal residence is Moscow's Great Kremlin Palace. Its massive red brick walls rise to the sky with bell towers and clock towers. Its huge, famous ruby-red stars can be seen from all directions in the city of Moscow. One entire side of the Kremlin is surrounded by the beautiful and historical Red Square, which includes St. Basil's Cathedral and Lenin's tomb. Another side of the Kremlin is encompassed with the lovely, tree-lined Alexandrovski Gardens.

At the far end of that Garden is a tall tower through which thousands of tourists enter every year to visit the State Armory Museum, one of the most fabulous museums in the entire world. As a person enters the State Armory Museum, he quickly becomes mesmerized as he walks past glass-enclosed dresses spun of pure silver that formerly adorned Russian queens. He can't help but be stunned by the dazzling crowns and regalia worn by the Russian monarchy.

As the onlooker is led along the museum corridors, he looks in amazement at thrones made of ivory, covered with diamonds or spiked with precious stones. With fascination he gapes at the gold-covered, diamond-encrusted carriages that once transported various branches of the Russian royal family.

But a favorite part of the museum, especially for men, is the section that displays the heavy metal armor that was once worn in battle hundreds of years ago. Behind walls of glass, one can look at hundreds of years of metal armor, including a huge horse that is dressed in heavy metal armor from medieval times. Every time I see this armor section of the museum, I think of Paul's words in Ephesians 6:11: "Put on the whole armor of God, that ye may be able to stand against the wiles of the devil."

The phrase "whole armor" is taken from the Greek word *panoplia,* and it refers *to a Roman soldier who is fully dressed in his armor from head to toe.* It is the word *pan,* which means all, combined with the word *hoplos,* which is the Greek word for *armor.* Together they form the word *panoplia,* which was officially recognized as the word to describe *the full attire and weaponry of a Roman soldier.*

Although not all-inclusive, the following list is the basic military hardware each soldier possessed:

Loinbelt

This was the central piece of weaponry that held much of the other pieces of armor in place. In Ephesians 6:14, Paul tells us that the believer is equipped with a loinbelt of truth, referring to the written Word of God.

Breastplate

This was a crucial piece of weaponry that defended the heart and the central organs of the body against attack. In Ephesians 6:14, Paul informs us that in our spiritual arsenal, we have at our disposal the "breastplate of righteousness."

Greaves

These specially formed pieces of metal were wrapped around the soldier's lower legs to protect him from being bruised and scraped and to defend his lower extremities from being hit hard and broken. In Ephesians 6:15, Paul refers to this vital piece of weaponry when he tells us that our feet are "...shod with the preparation of the gospel of peace."

Shoes

These heavy-duty shoes of a Roman soldier were covered with thick leather on the top and fitted with hobnails on the tip of the toe and the back of the heel. They were also heavily spiked with hobnails on their undersides. Paul makes reference to these shoes in Ephesians 6:15 when he talks about our feet being "...shod with the preparation of the gospel of peace."

Shield

The shield that the Roman soldier used in battle was long, door-shaped, and covered with leather hide. It was lubricated every day by the soldier to keep it soft and flexible so arrows that struck the shield would slide off and fall to the ground rather than penetrate it. In Ephesians 6:16, Paul declares that as a believer, you are specially outfitted with a "...shield of faith, wherewith ye shall be able to quench all the fiery darts of the wicked."

Helmet

The helmet of a Roman soldier, made either of brass or some other type of metal, was especially fitted to the shape of the soldier's head, thus protecting the head from receiving a mortal wound from an arrow, a sword, or an ax. In Ephesians 6:17, Paul proclaims the good news that God has provided every believer with "the helmet of salvation" to protect him against the mental assaults of the enemy.

Sword

The Roman soldier's sword, shaped similarly to a long dagger that was intended to be used in close battle, was absolutely indispensable to his ability to attack, overcome, and defeat his adversary. In Ephesians 6:17, we are taught by Paul that every believer has "...the sword of the Spirit, which is the word of God." This sword is God's Word, specially quickened inside us to use in times when we are in close combat with the adversary.

Lance

The lance gave the Roman soldier the ability to strike his enemy from a distance; therefore, no Roman soldier would be caught without his lance. Although Paul does not specifically mention the lance in his list of weaponry in Ephesians 6, it is suggested in verse 18 when Paul writes, "Praying always...." With the lance of prayer, each believer is able to assault the enemy from a distance, doing him so much damage that he is paralyzed in his attempts to come any nearer!

Because of Paul's many imprisonments, this was an easy illustration for Paul to use. Standing next to these illustrious soldiers during his prison internments, Paul could see the Roman soldier's *loinbelt; huge breastplate; brutal shoes affixed with spikes; massive, full-length shield; intricate helmet; piercing sword; and long, specially tooled lance that could be thrown a tremendous distance to hit the enemy from afar.*

Everything the soldier needed to successfully combat his adversary was at his disposal. Likewise, we have been given the whole armor of God — *everything* we need to successfully combat opposing forces. *Nothing is lacking!* Every piece of armor has great significance for us in our battle against an unseen enemy. God has provided everything you need to successfully stand up to the devil, to resist him, and to defeat him. Will you choose to obey or ignore Paul's urgent command to "put on the whole armor of God"? *Your success against an enemy that seeks every opportunity to destroy you depends on the choice you make!*

My Prayer for Today

Lord, how can I ever thank You enough for providing me with everything I need to successfully stand against each and every attack the devil tries to bring against my life? I thank You for loving me enough to equip me with these kinds of spiritual weapons. Because of what You have provided for me, I can stand fast, confident that I can withstand every assault, drive out the enemy, and win every battle. Without You, this would be impossible; but with Your power and the weapons You have provided for me, I am amply supplied with everything I need to push the enemy out of my way and out of my life! I pray this in Jesus' name!

My Confession for Today

I joyfully declare that I am dressed in the whole armor of God. There isn't a part of me that hasn't been supernaturally clothed and protected by the defensive and offensive weapons God has provided for me. I proceed with my loinbelt of truth; I walk in my shoes of peace; I boldly wear my breastplate of righteousness; I hold up my shield of faith; I am clad in my helmet of salvation; I make use of my sword of the Spirit; and I have a lance of intercession that deals a blow to the enemy from a distance every time I aggressively pray! I declare this by faith in Jesus' name!

Questions for You to Consider

1. How long has it been since you took time to stop and reflect on all the weaponry that God has provided for your defense and offense against the enemy?

   _____

   _____

   _____

   _____

   _____

   _____

2. Have you ever taken time to deeply study the spiritual weapons that God has supernaturally provided for you? If yes, what other steps can you take and what other books can you read to become better acquainted with this subject?

   _____

   _____

   _____

   _____

   _____

   _____

3. What did you learn from reading today's Sparkling Gem that you never realized before? After you think this question through and come up with the answer, why not share it with someone else today?

_____

_____

_____

_____

_____

_____

Day 31

Sword Power!

> *And take...the sword of the Spirit, which is the word of God.*
>
> — Ephesians 6:17

*H*ow would you like to deal a debilitating blow to the devil when he tries to attack your life and mind?

Today I want to talk to you about what Ephesians 6:17 calls the "sword of the Spirit" — a supernatural sword that has the power to drive back the enemy and deal a blow to his attacks against your life. When you have what I'm about to describe, it gives you *supernatural sword power* against the devil!

In Ephesians 6:17, Paul wrote, "And take...the sword of the Spirit, which is the word of God." In order to fully understand Paul's message regarding the sword of the Spirit, let's look at what the apostle had in his mind when he used the word translated "sword." It's the Greek word *machaira,* which is the very word used to describe the type of *sword* that Roman soldiers used in battle.

Because the Roman army was so committed to warfare, Roman soldiers continually practiced the arts of warfare. One daily exercise was sword practice, which they undertook both in the morning and the afternoon. Every soldier practiced sword fighting by striking a six-foot-high wooden post that was firmly fixed in the ground. This post became the soldier's "enemy" during practice. Just as he would if he were fighting a real enemy, the soldier would advance upon his target, strike hard with his sword, and then retreat.

The soldier's job in practice was to learn how to take advantage of his enemy, hit him at his weakest point, and strike him so he could not respond. His aim was nearly always directed toward the area of the post that represented the head or face, the thighs and legs, or occasionally the sides of the target.

The ancient Roman writer Vegetius described Roman sword-fighting tactics in his book *Concerning Military Matters,* saying, "They were likewise taught not to cut, but to thrust with their swords. For the Romans not only made jest of those who fought with the edge of that weapon, but always found them an easy conquest. A stroke with the edges, though, made with ever so much force, seldom kills, as the vital parts of the body are defended both by the bones and armor. On the contrary, a stab, though it penetrates but two inches, is generally fatal."[1]

The practices I just described are exactly what Paul had in mind when he wrote, "And take...the *sword* of the Spirit, which is the word of God" (Ephesians 6:17). How vital it is that we *understand* the sword of the Spirit!

Notice particularly where Paul said, "...the sword of the Spirit, which is the word of God." This word "word" is the Greek word *rhema,* which refers to a *specific, quickened word.* In order to have a sword that penetrates a blow to the enemy, we need a rhema — a specific, quickened word from the Scriptures —

placed into our hearts and mouths by the Holy Spirit. With a rhema from God placed in our hearts and mouths, we have *"sword power"*!

Remember, all a Roman soldier had to do in order to eradicate his enemies was make a well-placed, two-inch-deep stab wound. Likewise, one rhema from the Lord has the power to eliminate the enemy's attacks! *Thank God for the sword of the Spirit!*

The best example of this powerful sword of the Spirit is found in Luke 4:3-13. In this passage, Satan is repeatedly and aggressively attacking Jesus. But Jesus answered him repeatedly with a specific quickened *rhema* from the Holy Spirit. For example, after the devil tempted Jesus with food, Jesus drew the sword of the Spirit and rebuked Satan, saying, "...It is written, That man shall not live by bread alone, but by every word of God" (v. 4). *The enemy could not respond to this sword of the Spirit.*

When Satan offered Jesus all the kingdoms of the world in exchange for worship, Jesus drew another rhema and wounded him deeply yet again. Jesus said, "...it is written, Thou shalt worship the Lord thy God, and him only shalt thou serve" (v. 8). *To this sword of the Spirit, Satan had no answer.*

Finally, when Satan tempted Jesus to prove His deity, Jesus answered him again with a sword! He said, "It is said, Thou shalt not tempt the Lord thy God" (v. 12). With this *rhema,* Jesus penetrated Satan's armor with one final stab and dealt his enemy a devastating blow. Luke 4:13 tells us that after Jesus responded multiple times with a *rhema* — a specific, quickened word that dealt exactly with the type of attack Jesus was facing — the devil "departed" from him. Satan was nullified by these *rhema* words that Jesus drew and used like a spiritual sword against him.

Like the Lord Jesus, when the Holy Spirit quickens a scripture to you and you use it against the enemy, he will eventually "depart" from you because he has no answer with which to engage you in further combat. The sword of the Spirit is a supernatural spiritual weapon that renders the devil powerless. So today I want to urge you to open your heart to let the Holy Spirit reveal the exact scriptures you need to withstand the devil's attacks and to deal him a "fatal" blow. *With those scriptures in your heart and mouth, God will have given you a spiritual sword that the devil cannot resist!*

My Prayer for Today

Father, I am thankful for the ministry of the Holy Spirit. When I need sword power to stand against the enemy, the Holy Spirit quickens Scripture to my heart. When those verses are supernaturally revealed to me, please help me recognize and not forget or underestimate what is happening. Help me realize that the Spirit of God is placing a supernatural sword in my heart and that my job is to put it in my mouth and to wield it against the enemy. And, Father, just as the devil eventually "departed" from Jesus, at least for a season, I know that the devil will depart from me too. Thank You so much for the sword power that You give to me by the Spirit, quickening those verses to me at just the right time! I pray this in Jesus' name!

My Confession for Today

I confess that I have sword power to stand against the devil's attacks because the Holy Spirit quickens Scripture to my heart. When those verses are supernaturally quickened to me, the Spirit places a supernatural sword in my heart. As I release those words like a sword from my mouth, I wield a debilitating blow against the enemy. As I submit myself to God, I resist the devil and he must flee from me (James 4:7). I am thankful for the sword power that the Spirit gives to me and for quickening verses to me just in the right time! I declare this by faith in Jesus' name!

Questions for You to Consider

1. Can you think of a time when the Holy Spirit "quickened" a verse to you, and that verse gave you instant power to stand against the attacks that were being waged against you? What was the scripture that gave you *sword power* against the enemy? Have you continued to wield it against the enemy as part of your customized arsenal?

_____

_____

_____

_____

_____

2. If you are being attacked in your life or mind right now, have you asked the Holy Spirit to quicken a specific verse to you that will give you *sword power* against the devil's attacks?

_____

_____

_____

_____

_____

3. Do you know of any testimonies of someone who received a rhema word that suddenly gave that person direction and power for what he or she was doing or facing? What is that testimony?

Note

[1] Publius Flavius Vegetius Renatus, *Concerning Military Matters* (De Re Militari), Book I.

About Rick Renner

Rick Renner (**renner.org**) holds an earned ThD (Doctor of Theology) from a prominent Russian university and is a respected Bible teacher and leader in the international Christian community. He is the author of an extensive list of books, including bestsellers *Sparkling Gems From the Greek 1* and *2*, and his accumulated titles have sold millions of copies worldwide. Rick's understanding of the Greek language and biblical history opens up the Scriptures in a unique way that enables his audience to gain wisdom and insight while learning something brand new from the Word of God.

Today Rick is the overseer of the Good News Association of Churches, founder of the Moscow Good News Church, pastor of the Internet Good News Church, founder of Media Mir, and president of the Good News Channel — the largest Russian-speaking Christian satellite network in the world, which broadcasts the Gospel 24/7 to countless viewers in more than 83 nations. He is also founder of TBV, a national channel that broadcasts to all of Russia.

Rick is the founder of RENNER Ministries in Broken Arrow, Oklahoma, and host to his TV program, also seen around the world in multiple languages via television, Internet, and satellite. He leads this amazing work with Denise, his wife and lifelong ministry partner, along with their sons and committed leadership team.